UN STEADY DATING

PRaise foR
UNSteady DatiNg

"Absolutely perfect! JeaNette Smith has so completely hit the nail on the head with what young people need to know about dating and romance, I can't recommend it strongly enough! In a world gone completely crazy on this topic, *UNSteady Dating* sets the record straight with power, clarity, and humor . . . and in a way that preteens, teens, and young adults will eat up!"

—David Bowman
author and EFY presenter

"This is a an important book. It's engaging, fun, and was brought to life with real-life experiences. I loved it and highly recommend it to every teenager."

—John Hilton III
assistant professor at Brigham Young University

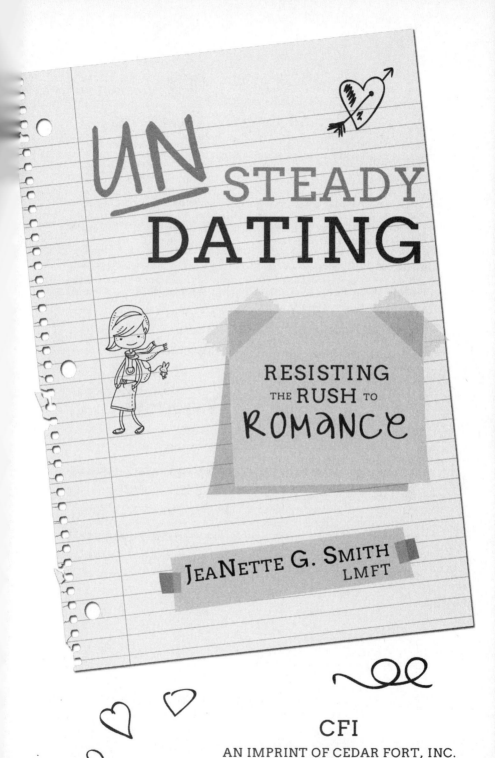

UN STEADY DATING

RESISTING THE RUSH TO ROMANCE

JeaNette G. Smith
LMFT

CFI

AN IMPRINT OF CEDAR FORT, INC.
SPRINGVILLE, UTAH

This is not an official publication of The Church of Jesus Christ of Latter-day Saints. The opinions and views expressed herein belong solely to the author and do not necessarily represent the opinions or views of Cedar Fort, Inc. Permission for the use of sources, graphics, and photos is also solely the responsibility of the author.

ISBN 13: 978-1-4621-1062-9

Published by CFI, an imprint of Cedar Fort, Inc.
2373 W. 700 S., Springville, UT 84663
Distributed by Cedar Fort, Inc., www.cedarfort.com

LIBRARY OF CONGRESS CATALOGING-IN-PUBLICATION DATA

Smith, JeaNette Goates, author.
 Unsteady dating : resisting the rush to romance / JeaNette Goates Smith.
  pages cm
 Summary: How to head off emotional or physical intimacy between dating teens and how to deal with it if either becomes an issue in teenagers' lives.
 Includes bibliographical references and index.
 ISBN 978-1-4621-1062-9 (alk. paper)
  1. Dating (Social customs)--Religious aspects--Church of Jesus Christ of Latter-day Saints. 2. Mormon youth--Conduct of life. 3. Parent and teenager--Religious aspects--Church of Jesus Christ of Latter-day Saints. I. Title.

BX8643.Y6S56 2012
241'.6765--dc23

                    2012010790

Cover design by Angela D. Olsen
Cover design © 2012 by Lyle Mortimer
Edited and typeset by Emily S. Chambers

Printed in the United States of America

10 9 8 7 6 5 4 3 2 1

Printed on acid-free paper

CONTENTS

CONTENTS

INtROduCtiON

Everybody's doing it. You can't walk down the halls at school without seeing couples with their arms draped around each other, holding hands, and even making out. High school romance is everywhere. You can't watch a movie with teenagers in it without seeing teenage romance glorified. It's as common as popcorn at the movies or hotdogs at a baseball game. It truly seems like everybody's doing it.

But when you think about it, everybody's doing lots of things. Everybody's watching R-rated movies, whether they sneak into the theatre or rent them online. Everybody's involved in underage drinking (3 out of 4 seniors in high school). Everybody smokes pot (actually only 1 in 5 seniors). And everybody has a boyfriend or girlfriend (1 in 3 is currently in a relationship). Since everybody's doing it, you might wonder what could possibly be wrong with it?

The youth in Zarahemla may have asked the same

question. There were so many people doing wicked things when Samuel the Lamanite came to preach that that there were barely enough righteous to save it. "Behold if it were not for the righteous who are in this great city, behold, I would cause that fire should come down out of heaven and destroy it" (Helaman 13: 13).

Just because so many high school students (it seems like everybody) have a boyfriend or girlfriend does not mean that pairing off in high school will bring you happiness.

President Hinckley counseled: "When you are young, do not get involved in steady dating. When you reach an age where you think of marriage, then is the time to become so involved. But you boys who are in high school don't need this, and neither do the girls."[1]

One of my sons—the one who attracted girls like mosquitoes—was shocked when I taught him not to have a girlfriend in high school. He looked around him, around the high school, at everybody he knew and told me, "Mom, you know you're trying to change the world."

"That's right, my dear," I responded. "It's time to change the world."

Endnotes

1. Gordon B. Hinckley, "Some Thoughts on Temples, Retention of Converts, and Missionary Service," *Ensign*, Nov. 1997.

Chapter 1

The FUNNel Theory

I SAW A MOVIE ONCE IN WHICH THE HERO TRAVELS BACK in time to the 1300s and rescues a girl to whom he is attracted. As they float down a river evading their pursuers, he asks, "Are you married?"

She replies, "No."

He asks, "Are you with anyone?"

She replies, "I'm with you."

He recognizes she doesn't understand his question and tries again, "Is there someone you're seeing?"

She replies, "No," then, scanning the nearby woods, adds, "Is it possible they are hiding on the shore?"

He then laughs and says, "We're speaking the same language, but you don't understand a word I'm saying, do you?"[1]

A similar level of confusion exists when discussing the subject of dating. It sometimes feels like we speak a different language—or that we are separated by ten centuries. Before we can even discuss teenage relationships, we have to speak the same language.

When we talk about "steady dating," we mean a couple has paired off; they are exclusive with one another; they refer to one another as boyfriend or girlfriend. To use Facebook terms, they are "in a relationship."

"Dating" at Sixteen

Whenever I speak to a youth group, I start off making sure we are speaking the same language. "When are you allowed to date?" I ask the audience. Everybody shouts out "sixteen." Then I ask the trick question. "When are you allowed to have a boyfriend or a girlfriend?"

And there is murmuring: "Didn't she just ask that question?", "What's the difference?"

Lots of youth think it's automatic: you turn sixteen, you date, and you get a boyfriend/girlfriend . . . *That's* what it means to date, lady. What century are *you* from?

Talking about "dating" is like talking about "love." The word has so many meanings, it's hard to know exactly what we are talking about. When we talk about love, we can talk about love for our fellow man, love for our family members, love for a romantic partner, and love for chocolate-covered almonds (which I absolutely adore). There are so many different kinds of love, it's a crime that we use the same word for such entirely different emotions.

The word "dating" is just as ambiguous. People who teach you about dating might talk about anything from how to put a napkin in your lap to how to keep your hands out of your date's lap.

The Funnel Theory

To clarify the different types of dating, I have created a model. When my kids are trying to explain something new to me (like how to use iMovie . . .), sometimes I don't get their point. In exasperation they will ask, "What do I need to do? Draw you a picture?" I'm a visual learner, so I enthusiastically respond, "Yes! That would be great!" Visual models make things so clear.

When I first presented this model, I used the shape of a solitaire-cut diamond, because diamonds represent love, engagement, commitment, and marriage—the very things the funnel theory is about. However, it's hard to draw a solitaire on the back of a napkin when you're sitting with your friends at an ice cream parlor, so I started using a funnel for convenience.

Some of the youth who saw the model when I first started teaching it have come up to me decades later, claiming they still remember it. In fact, many people simply refer to my presentation as "the Funnel Theory."

The diagram looks like a funnel—the kind you would use to pour oil into your automobile if you're brave enough to change your own oil (and not accidentally add oil to the transmission fluid). The top of the funnel represents the first stage of a relationship, and the bottom represents the last. As you progress through each stage of the funnel, your relationships become progressively more intimate.

The first stage of the funnel is the biggest stage because you include the most people in this stage. Each stage gets smaller because as you progress toward the end of the funnel, you include fewer numbers of people in each stage.

STAGE 1

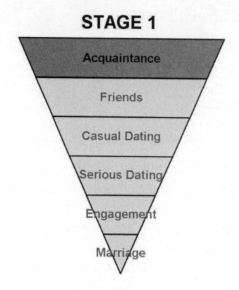

Stage One: Acquaintance

My husband and I like to go to the movies on our dates. I know some people think it's boring to do the same thing every weekend, but we don't think it's boring. We see a different movie each week! The ticket taker at our favorite theatre is an acquaintance. He is a darling young man who sits in a wheelchair as he tears our tickets. He doesn't know our names, but he smiles in recognition when he sees us. Most of us have lots and lots of acquaintances, so this stage is represented by the broadest part of the funnel.

A large part of your student body may be acquaintances to you, as are many of the members of your ward. You may or may not have anything in common with an acquaintance. You may or may not get along. If you do have things in common, and you do get along, an acquaintance may move into the next stage of the funnel: friendship.

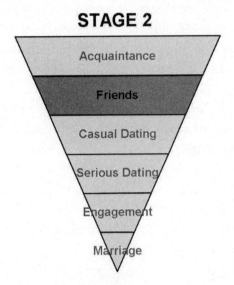

STAGE 2

Acquaintance

Friends

Casual Dating

Serious Dating

Engagement

Marriage

Stage Two: Friendship

Do not confuse Facebook friends with real friends. Nobody has 729 real friends. If you have hundreds and hundreds of "friends" on Facebook, they are actually fans or acquaintances, not friends.

A true friend is someone you care enough about that you will do more than just hit "like" when they send you and 728 other people a message. You care enough about your friends to actually call them on their birthdays or send a card, rather than just click a button.

We don't have nearly as many friends as we do acquaintances, so the friendship stage of our model is smaller in breadth as well as in depth than the first stage.

You will have lots of friends throughout the course of your life. You may have friends you go to church with, friends you play football with, friends you study with, friends from school, friends from other countries or cultures, and friends with varied political or religious beliefs. A friend is someone you care about, enjoy talking to, or enjoy spending time with. Some friends you have for a reason, some for a season, and some for a lifetime.

There is no reason to exclude someone from being a friend simply because they do not have your same beliefs. We can learn much from one another, can celebrate differences, and can become richer and more tolerant because we are friends with a variety of different people. However, if a supposed "friend" tries to persuade you to break the laws of the land, the laws of God, or even the Golden Rule, you might want to "unfriend" them.

STAGE 3

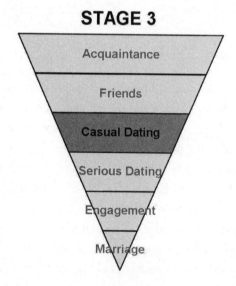

Stage Three: Casual Dating

When you go on a date with a friend who is a member of the opposite sex, we describe this as casual dating. Some of your friends will make it to this stage of the funnel, but certainly not the majority of them.

The funnel narrows a little more at this stage, reflecting the fact that the number of friends in this stage is smaller than in the previous stage. We have fewer friends in the "casual dating" stage than we have friends in general. You may have 20 or 30 friends in the friendship stage, but only 10–15 that you casually date.

We bring friends into the casual dating stage because we have more in common with them than with the wide variety of friends we had in stage two. We will be more inclined to casually date people with our same beliefs and values.

The casual dating stage, although a stage for your favorite friends, is still a *friendship* stage. This stage is exactly the same as stage two, except you are exclusive *for the duration of an event*. You aren't a couple and are not "in a relationship."

For example, my daughter was nominated to be on the homecoming court, which meant she was supposed to attend the homecoming dance, so she invited a friend from her social circle to be her "date" for the evening. You may have an extra ticket to a ballgame, so you invite a girl who is already a friend. You might want some company when you volunteer at the soup kitchen, so you invite a friend. You might invite a completely different friend the next time you have extra game tickets. You are not obligated in any way to begin "dating" someone just because you went on a "date."

In our society, particularly in the LDS culture, the moment a boy takes a girl out on a single date, all of the sudden they are "an item" or "a couple." They are "dating."

A perfect example of this is in the hilarious movie *Napoleon Dynamite*. Pedro takes the girl with the sideways ponytail to a dance, and the first thing Napoleon asks her is, "Are you and Pedro getting really serious now?"

The reason this is so funny is because it's so true. Teenagers are particularly guilty of creating a "couple" out of two people who have no intention of coupling. You find out that John asked Sarah out for Saturday night, and Sunday morning, everybody's heads are together, "Did you hear the news about John and Sarah?" Before you know it . . . before *they* even know it . . . the entire ward is anticipating a wedding announcement.

Casual dating occurs between young men and young women who have fun together; they have similar interests, however they are not romantically involved, and they are not exclusive. Casual dating is like playing ultimate Frisbee, tennis, or softball or any other sport. You're not going to say, "I only want to play with you, and I don't want you to play with anybody else. That would be childish. Likewise, in the casual dating stage, neither party tries to restrict the other's friendships.

STAGE 4

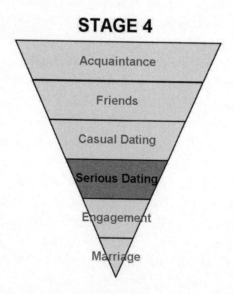

Acquaintance

Friends

Casual Dating

Serious Dating

Engagement

Marriage

Stage Four: Serious Dating

This is the stage you may think of when you think of dating. This is when you and someone you have been casually dating become exclusive. You decide to stop going out on dates with other people. You agree to be faithful to each other.

Serious dating is the same as steady dating. Therefore, we refer to casual dating as "unsteady" dating. Unsteady dating doesn't mean you wobble around on one leg, trying to avert a fall. Unsteady dating is simply the opposite of steady dating.

Because the word "dating" can be interpreted in so many ways, you may have been anticipating steady dating when your parents said, "You can't date until you're sixteen." In reality, you begin casual dating at sixteen, and your relationships with members of the opposite sex are not a lot different than they were when you were twelve, or fourteen. Serious dating doesn't begin until you are in a position to marry. For the girls, that won't occur until you are out of high school, at the very earliest, and for the boys, that won't occur until you return from your missions.

For those of you who are disappointed, please don't be. As you'll see throughout this book, you can have way more fun casual dating in your teenage years then you ever would serious dating. You'll find you're a lot happier, way less stressed, and seriously excited about life.

STAGE 5

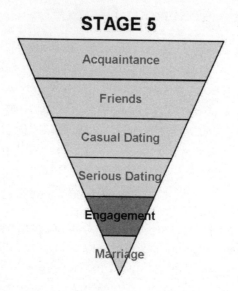

Acquaintance

Friends

Casual Dating

Serious Dating

Engagement

Marriage

Stage Five: Engagement

After you have dated seriously for a while, you will know whether you want to spend the rest of your life, and eternity too, with this person. You are exclusive with one another and determined not to be with any other member of the opposite sex romantically ever again. You are in love and decide to marry. You make a verbal commitment to one another, often symbolized by the gift of an engagement ring.

This is the first stage in which it is appropriate to formalize your relationship with a ring. Young people who want to formalize their commitment with a promise ring are making the very mistake they need to avoid—getting serious when they are in no position to marry. Promises made in high school are meant to be broken. Statistically, there is little or no chance that you will keep those promises to one another, and you have no business making them. It is therefore inappropriate to wear a promise ring.

The engagement stage of a relationship is narrower than the serious dating stage, which was narrower than the casual dating stage. The number of people who make it into the engagement stage of a relationship is the smallest yet.

Of the 10–15 friends you might consider dating casually, only a handful, if even that many, should be considered for serious dating. (Remember, if you date five people seriously, then you will have had to break up with four of them.) Then, of the five or so people you have dated seriously, only one or two will ever enter into the engagement stage. The hope is that only one will enter the engagement stage because, again, a breakup of a relationship when the expectation was marriage, is more painful than a breakup with lower expectations. A breakup during the engagement stage will disappoint not only the couple but also all the family members, friends, and caterers and florists who were excited about the marriage.

STAGE 6

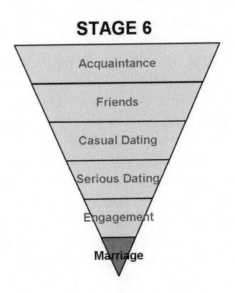

Stage Six: Marriage

The ultimate stage of the relationship model is marriage. Of all the friends we make, of all the people we date casually and then date seriously, only one person will make it all the way to the marriage stage. If you get divorced, then there may be more than one person who makes it to the marriage stage, but divorce is exactly what we're trying to prevent with the Funnel Theory. If the pain of a breakup during the serious dating stage is large, and the pain during engagement even larger, imagine the pain if a marriage breaks up. Then the caterer is the least of the disappointed. Children and extended family members may be devastated for decades.

A successful, lasting marriage occurs when we experience *each and every* stage of the funnel. Marriages are stronger when couples begin their relationships with a foundation of friendship. Marriages are stronger when couples refuse to rush into serious dating and instead date casually until they are in a position to marry. Marriages are stronger when each member of the couple has done his or her homework and has gotten to know lots of people, lots of personalities, and lots about themselves before they decide to settle down with one person.

Marriage is the culmination of years of hard work. It takes *time* to make friends with a number of people. It takes *discipline* to select a few people from those you call friends and to date them only casually. From the selection of people you date casually, it takes *discernment* to decide whom you want to date seriously. When you do find someone with whom you believe you could happily spend the rest of your life, your discipline and discernment will have paid off, and you will have a delightful, fulfilling marriage.

Endnotes

1. *Timeline*, 2003.

Chapter 2

ONLY YOU...FOREVER

DID YOU NOTICE THAT THE FIRST THREE STAGES OF the funnel in the Funnel Theory are all friendship stages? Acquaintances, friends, and people you casually date are in an entirely different category than those in the last three stages of the funnel. The last three stages, steady dating, engagement, and marriage, are romance stages. You like people in the first three stages, but you *love* those that make it into one of the last three stages. Your love grows as you progress to an ever more serious stage, but the break—the shift from like to love, from friendship to romance—occurs when you switch from casual dating to serious dating. There is a big difference between the friendship stages and the romance stages. Many hearts get broken when a couple isn't on the same page about moving from friendship to romance.

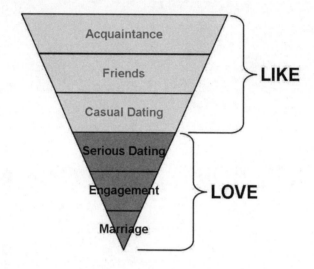

A boy and a girl were having dinner at a restaurant, and one of their friends saw them and came over. She asked, "How long have you guys been dating?" They both respond *simultaneously*: "Oh, we're not dating," the boy says.

At the very same time the girl says, "About two weeks."

Clearly there is confusion, even within the relationship, as to what stage they are in. The girl thinks they are in an exclusive relationship. She's totally into it. The boy thinks differently.

Moving from like to love is a big deal. You can't just fall in love. It's too important to let happen by accident. You have to be ready for the responsibility of a loving relationship. When you go steady, you are putting yourself in a position to be in love. You're too smart to give your heart to someone if you're not going steady, but if there's a promise of exclusivity, you'll give it away.

Two conditions exist in a romance that don't exist in a friendship. These two conditions are what give you the courage to give away your heart. The two elements that exist in romance that don't exist in a friendship are *exclusivity* and *commitment*. Exclusivity means, "I will be faithful to you," and commitment means, "I will never leave you." That's pretty romantic, isn't it? It's no wonder the illusion of exclusivity and commitment enable you to move from like to love.

When exclusivity and commitment are present in a relationship, we can let our guard down and feel free to love without getting hurt. We give these two things to a romantic relationship and expect them from a romantic relationship. We don't give these same two things to a friendship and don't expect them from a friendship.

Without exclusivity and commitment, you won't give your heart away. Yet, when you believe you are in an exclusive, committed relationship, you can love with all your heart. By definition, steady dating is an exclusive relationship, which leads some to believe it's safe to give your heart away. This stage, however, does not always include commitment.

When *Not* to Expect Exclusivity

Notice that in the first three stages of a relationship, there is no exclusivity. There's not supposed to be. People who are mere acquaintances do not expect you to have relationship with just them. That would be psycho. There's actually a name for that kind of mental illness. It is called Borderline Personality Disorder. If you come across an acquaintance who feels entitled to have you all to him-or herself, realize this is not normal behavior and try to get out of the situation.

Even in stages two and three, when people are just

friends, they should not expect exclusivity. Maybe when you were six years old, you got jealous if your friend played with another friend. However, you're not six anymore. Healthy friendships leave room for relationships with other people. Friends don't have to spend every waking minute together. They don't have to attend every social event together. Friends don't get jealous when one of them has other plans with another friend. Exclusivity is inappropriate in a grown-up friendship.

Even "best friends" will soon smother one another if they are so possessive that they do not allow the other to be friends with anybody else. In a healthy friendship, the friends give one another space to develop other relationships.

In the casual dating stage, which is a friendship stage, you can expect temporary exclusivity. If a guy asks you to a dance, you can expect him to spend his time with you throughout the evening and not ditch you to be with someone else. But you can't expect to be exclusive the next day or the next weekend. Your relationship is not exclusive.

Elder Oaks has encouraged those who are not yet in exclusive relationships not to make such a big deal about dates. When you are casually dating, just lighten up.

The more elaborate and expensive the date, the fewer the dates. As dates become fewer and more elaborate, this seems to create an expectation that a date implies seriousness or continuing commitment. That expectation discourages dating even more . . .

Simple and more frequent dates allow both men and women to "shop around" in a way that allows extensive evaluation of the prospects. The old-fashioned date was a wonderful way to get acquainted with a member of the opposite sex. It encouraged conversation. It allowed you to see how you treat others and how you are treated in a one-on-one situation. It gave opportunities to learn how to initiate and sustain a mature relationship. [1]

When Exclusivity Is a *Must*

On the other hand, there are big changes that occur when you decide to move from a casual dating stage to a serious dating stage. Big changes. In the serious dating stage, two people, who were previously just friends, are now more-than-friends. They are "boyfriend" and "girlfriend."

Teens who decide to "go together" think they can manage an exclusive relationship, but they can't. One of the reasons high school students' romances fail is that teens want the privilege of a boyfriend or girlfriend, but they really don't want to settle down. They want to flirt, post on other's Facebook page, and show interest in or hang out with members of the opposite sex. From what I've observed, cheating is the most common reason high school romances break up. What was supposedly an exclusive relationship, wasn't.

Anthropologist Helen Fisher found that couples in a "serious" relationship demand exclusivity. "They do not wish to have their 'sacred' relationship sullied by outsiders." Fisher continues, "Once a man or woman falls in love and begins to yearn for emotional union with a sweetheart, they profoundly want this mate to remain sexually faithful—to them." [2]

Teenagers don't handle it very well when they get cheated on. (Neither do some adults, I might add.) I have a client (not LDS) whose boyfriend keyed her car when she said she wanted to see other people. She reported the incident to the police and paid a lot of money to have the car repainted. As soon as her boyfriend saw the new paint job, he keyed the car again.

You have probably heard the song, "Before He Cheats" by Carrie Underwood. She sings, "I dug my key into the side of his pretty little souped up four-wheel drive." This from a woman who was surprised that her beloved cheated on her. But when she discovered his true character she determined, "the next time he cheats, it won't be on me . . ."

I'm not suggesting you get a boyfriend or girlfriend and not cheat. I'm saying don't get a boyfriend or girlfriend until you're old enough that you won't *want* to cheat. Have lots of friendships in high school, and don't go steady with anyone until you are truly ready to be exclusive.

When you decide to have a romantic relationship, you need to know that romance comes with a price. The price of romance is exclusivity. You can't be expected to give your heart away, to love with all your heart, unless your beloved will take good care of that heart. Therefore, if a young man thinks he wants to experience romance (and likewise a young woman) he better make sure he is ready to be in an exclusive relationship. That means no cheating. No flirting. Love is something that can't be trifled with. If a young person wants the privilege of love, he or she better be ready for the responsibility of exclusivity.

"Love is a fragile thing," says Jeffrey R. Holland in his essay, "and some elements in life can try to break it. Much damage can be done if we are not in tender hands, caring hands. I want to impress upon you the vulnerability and delicacy of your partner's future as it is placed in your hands for safekeeping—male and female, it works both ways."[3]

One of the things I kind of like about Facebook is that it keeps people honest. You can't pretend you're serious and faithful to someone's face and then go flirting around behind his or her back. Your relationship status tells everybody whether you're allowed to flirt or not. If you go around flirting and your status says "in a relationship," everybody you know will be posting photos of you flirting with somebody you're not in a relationship with, and within minutes you are busted!

When *Not* to Expect Commitment

While exclusivity means "I will be faithful to you," commitment means "I will never leave you."

When you enter the romance stages of a relationship—steady dating, engagement, and marriage—you are entitled, not only to exclusivity, you are entitled to commitment.

While serious dating doesn't warrant the same commitment as engagement or marriage, it deserves the *intention* to commit. You don't enter the steady dating stage *expecting* to break up. You enter thinking that there may be a real possibility that you will stay together. Too often high school students enter the serious dating stage fully intending to break up. They know there are more fish in the sea. They anticipate they will get bored, lose interest, or grow restless. They fully plan to leave as soon as someone cuter, richer, smarter, or more fun comes along.

Some of my friends in Florida call this "serial monogamy." They believe that in a romantic relationship you have to be exclusive, but you don't have to make a commitment. You have to be exclusive while you're dating, but you can break up at any time for any reason. Once you break up, you are free to talk with, flirt with, and go out on dates with whomever you wish.

If you're going to get serious, you at least have to want to stay together. You have to give the relationship your best shot.

There is nothing meaner than allowing someone to fall in love with you, knowing full well you are going to leave them when it becomes convenient. Someone who convinces you to give away your heart, being fully aware he or she will eventually leave you, is a creep. Or you might call him or her a player, a rake, or a wag. There are lots of these types of characters throughout literature. Beware of them! It is deceitful for someone to enter the serious dating stage while not intending from the start for it to last.

Also foolish and hurtful, though not quite as creepy, some high school students enter the steady dating stage when they do not have the *ability* to commit. They may want to stay together, but the possibility is really slim. They have too much living yet to do. If you know full well that you will probably break up when one of you goes off to college or goes on a mission, you have absolutely no business entering into the steady dating stage. Do not make a commitment you may not be able to keep. It's like selling stock you don't own.

Exclusivity without Commitment

Sometimes we refer to the type of relationship where youth are exclusive but not committed as "puppy love." Puppy love is a relationship where a couple truly loves one another, but they are in no position to make a commitment. Don't be deceived by the term puppy love. It does not mean the love is weak or soft or insignificant. Youth who become exclusive can develop deep feelings for one another, and just because they know they can't do anything about those feelings does not mean the feelings aren't poignant and real.

Puppy love, or exclusivity without commitment, is

a recipe for heartbreak. Two people are in an exclusive relationship, which naturally fosters loving feelings, but they are no position to commit because they are so young and have so much living left to do before they marry.

Some of that living young men have left to do before they marry is to serve a mission. This is one of the reasons prophets and church leaders advise against going steady in high school. You are in no position to make commitments to each other. You can't stay together even if you want to. It is not the appropriate time to make a commitment to a girl. It is the time to make a commitment to the Lord to teach the gospel for two years. The commitment young men make to the Lord will clash with a commitment they want to make to a young lady. Too often, young men who get too serious before their missions choose the young lady and sacrifice their commitment to the Lord.

One time, a dear friend of mine called me, sobbing uncontrollably because her son had elected not to serve a mission. He had gotten serious with a young lady, and she declared she couldn't live without him for two years and asked him not to go on his mission. I thought my friend would never stop crying.

Still, full of faith, my friend decided they would fast as a family. The entire family came to church on the day of the fast and sat in the back of the chapel. Throughout the meeting, the missionary-age son sat defiantly with his arms crossed over his chest. Finally, it was time for the closing song. As the congregation joined in singing the words to "I'll Go Where You Want Me to Go," it was the missionary-aged son who began weeping. His arms fell to his side, and his head dropped into his lap. Throughout the song, his heaving body assured my friend that her prayer had been answered. Her son changed his mind. He told his girlfriend good-bye, and he kept his commitment to the Lord. He turned in his missionary papers and served a faithful, focused mission.

True Commitment

One of my favorite fictional characters is Horton in Dr. Seuss's *Horton Hatches the Egg*. In it, the bird Lazy Daisy Mae leaves her egg behind in the care of Horton, a passerby elephant. Despite the bird being gone for far longer than she said, Horton sits on that egg come rain, come snow, come hunters with guns. Horton says, "I meant what I said / And I said what I meant . . . / An elephant's faithful / One hundred per cent." [4] I want Hortons in my life. There's an elephant I would trust. Horton knows how to keep a commitment. I hope you surround yourself with Hortons.

Karl G. Maeser helps us understand what it means to make a commitment. "I have been asked what I mean by my word of honor. I will tell you. Place me behind prison walls—walls of stone ever so high, ever so thick, reaching ever so far into the ground—there is a possibility that in some way or another I may be able to escape, but stand me on that floor and draw a chalk line around me and have me give my word of honor never to cross it. Can I get out of that circle? No, never! I'd die first!" [5]

I'm always amazed at the power of a covenant as illustrated in the Book of Mormon. Moroni captures Zerahemnah, the commander of the Lamanite armies, and offers to let him and all his troops go scot free, if they will make a covenant to lay down their weapons of war and never come to battle again. Zerahemnah could have lied. He could have simply said, "sure" and been on his way. But even in battle, even with his life at stake, Zerahemnah would not make an oath he knew he would break.

> And now it came to pass that when Zerahemnah had heard these sayings he came forth and delivered up his sword and his cimeter, and his bow into the hands of Moroni, and said unto him: Behold, here are our weapons of war; we will deliver them up unto you, but we will not suffer ourselves to take an oath unto you, which we know that we shall break, and also our children; but take our weapons of war, and suffer that we may depart into the wilderness; otherwise we will retain our swords, and we will perish or conquer. (Alma 44:8)

You might not admire the Lamanites' politics, but you have to admire their commitment. They refuse to make a promise they know they can't keep.

The ability to keep a commitment is a sign of maturity. Marriage is the stage in which commitment to a relationship is absolutely crucial. When a relationship gets rough, sometimes the commitment is the only thing that keeps a couple together. Anybody who expects a commitment like that from a high school student has been listening to too much Taylor Swift.

Endnotes

1. Dallin H. Oaks, "The Dedication of a Lifetime," CES Fireside for Young Adults, May 1, 2005.

2. Helen Fisher, *Why We Love: The Nature and Chemistry of Romantic Love.* New York: Henry Holt and Company, 2004, 20-21.

3. Jeffrey R. Holland, "How Do I Love Thee?" Brigham

Young University Speeches, February 15, 2000.

4. Dr. Seuss, *Horton Hatches the Egg*, New York: Random House, 1910.

5. Karl G. Maeser, "The Circle of Honor," Brigham Young University Honor Code brochure, 2002.

Chapter 3

Emotional Intimacy

EVERY STAGE OF A RELATIONSHIP IN THE FUNNEL Theory is a wonderful stage. They are all good, appropriate, and righteous. We all have acquaintances. It's delightful to have friends. It's wonderful to casually date. It's necessary to seriously date, and it's God's plan for you to become engaged and to marry. There is nothing wrong with any of these stages. The crucial question is timing.

When I was eight years old I wanted only one thing for my birthday. I wanted a little travel bag that I could fill with pj's when I slept over at a friend's house or went to visit my grandma. For weeks and weeks before my birthday, I dropped obvious hints, so no one would have any doubts about what to get me for my birthday.

Three weeks before my birthday, my little sister who was turning six had a birthday. Lo and behold, when she blew out her candles and tore the wrapping paper off her gift, she had the very gift I had wanted. She received a small canvas bag, patterned with autumn-colored flowers, and had a pocket on the outside and a tiny lock to connect the zipper that opened the bag.

I was green with envy. I was so upset that my little sister had received *my* gift that I couldn't think of anything else. I cried out, "That's not fair! I was the one who wanted an overnight bag! Becky didn't even want one. Why is she the one who got the bag?" Finally, fed up with my whining, my mother dove into her walk-in closet, and from the very back, underneath stacks of shoes, she pulled out another canvas overnight bag.

"Here," she thrust the bag at me. "If you want it so bad, take it. I hope you're happy." I stared at the bag, which was exactly like my sister's, except the flowers were in shades of red and purple. It was just what I wanted, and I felt terrible. I had wanted the bag but not under those circumstances. I wanted candles and a cake, and I wanted people to sing "Happy Birthday" to me. I wanted to pull off the bow and tear apart the wrapping paper. I wanted it to be a celebration. Instead, it was devastating. I was ashamed. I felt alone. I felt stupid.

I have since thought how tragic it was that a gift that could have brought me so much joy, brought me so much sorrow. If I had only waited. If I had just been patient. I could have had exactly what I wanted, and it would have been a celebration rather than a disappointment.

A few years ago, Elder Dallin H. Oaks gave a wonderful talk entitled "Timing." In it he says, "In all the important decisions in our lives, what is most important is to *do the right thing*. Second, and only slightly behind the first, is to *do the right thing at the right time*. People who do the right thing at the wrong time can be frustrated and ineffective. They can even be confused about whether they made the right choice when what was wrong was not their choice but their timing."[1]

Going steady is the right thing. Going steady in high school is the wrong timing. When you are encouraged to date at sixteen, that means to casually date, not to seriously date. It means to go on a date, not get a boyfriend or a girlfriend.

Why Wait?

When you spend time in an exclusive relationship, before you know it, you will find yourself falling in love. It happens all the time. You have seen all kinds of movies in which this happens, even when the couple doesn't want it to happen.

The classic movie *The Princess Bride* tells of a young girl who falls in love with her servant. There are class distinctions that make this an unlikely match that the couple would not deliberately seek. Nevertheless, after spending so much time together (and after Wesley proves himself exceptionally loyal and doting), they grow to love one another.

The Sound of Music, another classic, tells of similar alliance. Captain Von Trapp would never deliberately seek a mere governess as a mate. Nevertheless, after spending time with her and getting to know her, he discovers he is quite attracted to Maria and she to him. A beautiful love story unfolds.

When your feelings for someone grow deeper and deeper, you develop emotional intimacy. Intimacy means you're close. Emotional intimacy means your hearts are close, or you are in love.

While emotional intimacy, or romantic love, is

wonderful and desirable and maybe one of the best things in life, it's not all that wonderful in high school. One of the problems with falling in love in high school is that emotional intimacy leads to physical intimacy.

Youth who would never consider indulging in physical intimacy develop an entirely different mindset when they enter into a serious relationship. When youth form exclusive, loving relationships, sex seems like the natural thing to do. It doesn't seem as taboo when they are "in love." Like one LDS young man who had come to me for counseling said, "We felt like we were married, so we figured we could act like we were married."

A Brigham Young University study of fifty unwed mothers discovered that only one had engaged in sexual relations because it felt good physically. Ninety-eight percent of the girls interviewed gave emotional reasons for engaging in premarital sex.

Scientists clearly recognize that the more time a couple spends exclusively with one another, the more likely it is that their friendship will become a romance. "Before the relationship grows into romantic love, you may feel attracted to several individuals, directing your attention to one, then another. But eventually you begin to concentrate your passion on just one. This phenomenon is related to the human inability to feel romantic passion for more than one person at a time."[2]

Physical intimacy is a natural, normal, and healthy result of emotional intimacy. People who "fall in love" desire to "make love." Teenagers who "fall in love" desire to "make love." In a survey conducted for her book *How We Love*, anthropologist Helen Fisher found that a substantial 73 percent of men and 65 percent of women daydreamed about having sex with the one they love.[3]

My daughter always says, "It's stupid to think we have that much control as teenagers. We barely have the discipline to wake up for early morning seminary. We shouldn't be so proud that we think we are stronger than everybody else."

Prophets have warned us about the connection between emotional intimacy and physical intimacy. President Gordon B. Hinckley said, "It is better, my friends, to date a variety of companions until you are ready to marry. Have a wonderful time, but stay away from familiarity. . . . Steady dating at an early age leads so often to tragedy. Studies have shown that the longer a boy and girl date one another, the more likely they are to get into trouble." [4]

If you truly want to remain abstinent until marriage, you need to look at what comes *before* sexual intimacy. What happens in your head will determine what you do with your hands. Proverbs teaches, "As [a man] thinketh in his heart, so is he" (23:7). The scriptures warn that we must watch our thoughts, and words and deeds (Mosiah 4:30). Because our thoughts precede our deeds, we can avoid sexual intimacy by being careful with what happens before the sexual intimacy: emotional intimacy.

Please Forgive Us

Admittedly, you have been getting double-messages on this topic. Some adults wink at your emotionally intimate relationships and in the same breath tell you not to go "too far" physically. Some adults may not merely tolerate but actually encourage your romantic relationships. This isn't fair to you. It is unrealistic to encourage emotionally intimate relationships and then at the same time expect you to avoid physically intimate relationships.

You may think waiting to date until you turn sixteen is enough to keep you out of emotionally intimate relationships. It is not. Two things are wrong with this idea: Youth find a way to become emotionally intimate, even if they are technically not allowed to "date." They communicate endlessly through texting, Facebook, or email. Sometimes they even use the telephone. A couple can be seriously committed to one another, perhaps even love one another without ever going on a date. If they happen to be at the same event, at youth conference, or at a joint activity, they'll sneak away together and pursue their romance.

Brent Top tells the story of a young woman who came to see the bishop because she was pregnant out of wedlock. The bishop asked her how old she was when she began to date. She told the bishop, "I do not date. I follow the prophet's counsel."[5] Clearly, she had never been taught about emotionally intimate relationships. You can definitely get too intimate without ever going on a date.

The second danger of relying on the "you can't date until you're sixteen" mantra is that you think that turning sixteen is a really big deal—some magical world where you are suddenly old enough to find love and romance. So you may postpone your emotionally intimate relationships until age sixteen, but then suddenly all bets are off. You're ready to find a boyfriend or girlfriend and you jump right into an emotionally intimate relationship.

In a conference address, Elder Larry Lawrence gave the following counsel:

> Parents can prevent a lot of heartache by teaching their children to postpone romantic relationships until the time comes when they are ready for

marriage. Prematurely pairing off with a boyfriend or girlfriend is dangerous. Becoming a couple creates emotional intimacy, which too often leads to physical intimacy. Satan knows this sequence and uses it to his advantage. He will do whatever he can to keep young men from serving missions and to prevent temple marriages.[6]

Emotionally intimate relationships simply are not appropriate for high school. One of the crucial reasons is that it's so easy to become physically intimate. Physical intimacy, however, isn't the *only* danger of emotionally intimate relationships. Even if you manage to completely avoid physical intimacy, high school romance is still a rotten idea. Premature emotional intimacy itself can ruin your high school years, compromise a mission, and—even more tragic—damage your eventual marriage.

Endnotes

1. Dallin Oaks, "Timing," BYU Devotional Speeches, Jan. 29, 2002. Emphasis added.

2. Helen Fisher, *Why We Love: The Nature and Chemistry of Romantic Love*. New York: Henry Holt and Company, 2004, 6.

3. Ibid., 20.

4. Gordon B. Hinckley, "A Prophet's Counsel and Prayer for Youth," *Ensign*, Jan. 2001, 2.

5. Brent Top, Brigham Young University, Education Week, Aug. 16, 1999.

6. Larry Lawrence, "Courageous Parenting," *Ensign*, Nov. 2010.

Chapter 4

The POWeR Of TOUCh

Y**OU JUST LEARNED THAT EMOTIONAL INTIMACY LEADS** to physical intimacy. The hope is that if you avoid emotional intimacy, you will naturally avoid physical intimacy. Interestingly, it works the other way around too. Physical intimacy also leads to emotional intimacy.

Many people, teenagers and adults alike, don't want this to be true. They want to indulge in physical intimacy, and then they want to walk away without any emotional connection whatsoever. They think they can use each other, fool around, go their separate ways, and never look back. Nope. Doesn't work that way.

People who like physical intimacy but don't want a relationship try to make it seem acceptable by putting a clever label on it: "make-out buddy," or "friends with benefits," they want to call it. Let me tell you something important: there is no such thing. There is no such thing as friends with benefits. A true friend would not use you and then toss you away. Just because you agree to the arrangement, just because you are supposed to be getting something out of it too, does not mean it is a kind way to treat one another. It is not what real friends do.

The problem with the view that sex can be a physical act without any other ramifications is that it has no supporting evidence either in anecdotal surveys or in scientific research. Even if you have convinced yourself that you can have sexual relations with someone and it means nothing, it is *still* relational. This is true for both women and men, debunking the stereotype that men can have sex with no emotional or relational consequences.[1]

The Power of Touch

Touch is a powerful thing. My dad used to tell a story that happened to him in medical school. He was working in the neonatal intensive care unit (NICU), where they care for preemie babies. One time a little Mexican-American baby was born and was failing to thrive. All his vital signs had been gradually getting worse, and it became apparent this baby was going to die. My dad stood by the tiny body one day, wondering what more they could do for him. The baby lay on his tummy with his knees tucked under his chest. My dad knew he may never see this baby alive again and placed his hand in the isolette, gently stroked his fingers down the tiny spine. For several minutes he tenderly touched the tiny body, quietly saying good-bye before he continued on his rounds.

The next day, Dad returned to the NICU and to his amazement, the baby was still there. Not only was he alive, but his vital signs were better. He had actually improved. Dad developed a fondness for this baby and continued to visit, and although the infant couldn't be held, Dad could touch him. Daily he ran his fingers tenderly down the tiny back, gently stroking, communicating affection without words. The baby continued to improve and within weeks was well. He was soon able to leave the hospital and go home with his family.

Since that time, scientific studies have been conducted that validate the necessity of touch in human survival. Touch is important no matter what your age.

Several years ago my husband was serving as the bishop of our ward. He already had a demanding career and was now working valiantly to save a struggling ward as well. I tell the following story in my book *Side by Side*.

"At 9:00 one Sunday evening my husband walked through the door. His tie hung loosely around his unbuttoned collar, and his hair was disheveled.

"How was your day?" I asked cheerily.

"I need a stair hug" is all he said.

I scuttled to the staircase and stepped up one stair. I was then almost tall enough to look him in the eyes. He wrapped his arms around me, rested his head on my shoulder, and didn't say a word." [2]

Whatever was troubling him (I don't know what it was), a long, focused embrace was enough to make him feel better. I have actually seen T-shirts that have "I need a hug" printed on the front. Several years ago, a movement started where people offered "free hugs" to strangers. They would literally stand in a plaza and hold a sign that said "free hugs." People looked at them like they were totally weird at first, and then began taking advantage of the free hugs.

Juan Mann describes his inspiration for this hug movement as follows:

Standing there in the arrivals terminal, watching other passengers meeting their waiting friends and family, with open arms and smiling faces, hugging and laughing together, I wanted someone out there to be waiting for me. To be happy to see me. To smile at me. To hug me. So I got some cardboard and a marker and made a sign. I found the busiest pedestrian intersection in the city and held that sign aloft, with the words "Free Hugs" on both sides.

And for 15 minutes, people just stared right through me. The first person who stopped, tapped me on the shoulder and told me how her dog had just died that morning. How that morning had been the one year anniversary of her only daughter dying in a car accident. How what she needed now, when she felt most alone in the world, was a hug. I got down on one knee, we put our arms around each other and when we parted, she was smiling.[3]

If a hug sends such a powerful message of caring and concern, can you imagine what happens when you kiss?

The Power of a Kiss

Some youth will justify kissing based on the argument that both of them know that kissing doesn't imply commitment. However, kissing is so intrinsically bonding that even if youth think they can do it casually, they will soon find they have given away something that meant more to them then they thought it did. Kissing turned out to be an intimate behavior belonging in an exclusive relationship after all.

Van Epp says, "Sex and self are inextricably linked, and during a sexual encounter something happens that is more than just a physical act."[4]

Here is what couples reported happened to them emotionally, as a result of the physical intimacy:

- Stronger desire to open up

- Desire to feel closer

- Feeling of vulnerability

- Apprehension about letting down their guard

- An increase in overall need for the other partner

- Wanting to spend more time with one another

- Pulled toward dependency[5]

Sometimes I work with young adults who are having a difficult time finding someone to marry. They feel pressure because they are old enough but just haven't found someone that really makes their heart flutter. When I'm teaching young adults, I tell them just the opposite of what I'm teaching you. I encourage them to take a chance in their relationships: start to kiss. If everything else is working in the relationship, they are both in a position to marry, they both have similar values, they are good friends, they get along, and all you need is a spark, then kiss, for heaven's sake.

Kissing is *supposed* to bring you closer as a couple. It's supposed to help you fall in love. Just like intercourse after marriage is supposed to bond you even further. Physical intimacy leads to emotional intimacy. That's part of the plan. It's just not the part of the plan you're experiencing in high school.

Communicating through Touch

Physical intimacy is important for another reason: it communicates to your partner what you think of them. It tells your partner how serious you are about the relationship.

Those of you who are fans of chick flicks (and those who get dragged to them) recognize *Titanic* as one of the most engaging love stories in recent years. In this movie, the directors know precisely how to use touch to communicate the depth of a relationship. In the famous scene where Kate leans trustingly into Jack's arms as they embrace the wind at the bow of the ship, we know, that the moment their outstretched arms touch and their fingers intertwine, their friendship has turned into a love affair.

We've been raised on fairy tales with similar relationship clues. The handsome prince spots Cinderella the moment she enters the room. His eyes follow her down the staircase as his feet scurry to intercept her wanderings. They dance, they talk, they stare into one another's eyes, and finally, they kiss. Whew. Now we know they are in love. They will marry and live happily ever after.

Consider how disappointed we would be if they didn't kiss! What if he shook her hand and said "good-bye." Or what if he waved or bowed? You'd be on the edge of your seat. "How does he feel? Didn't he like her? What's going to happen?" We have no assurance of a happy ending. We have no indication that this woman is any different than any of the other beautiful women attending the ball. The kiss on the mouth tells us everything. In our culture we express love—romantic love—through physical touch.

The prince kisses Snow White to reveal his true love, thus bringing her to back to life, and a subsequent marriage. Sleeping Beauty is awakened from her long sleep with a kiss from her handsome prince, who of course, then marries her. The Beast is saved from death by Beauty's kiss. Ariel in Disney's *Little Mermaid* is freed from the spell from Ursula only by a kiss from her beloved. If we don't see a kiss in fairy tales, how would we know if there is love?

A kiss on the lips communicates that you are exclusive. Don't pretend it doesn't. If your date drops you off on the front porch and you get a kiss good night, you're pretty sure he's going to ask you out again. If he drops you off and gives you a hug, you're not always sure.

Why do you think that's the first thing all your friends ask you after a date? Did he kiss you? Did you kiss her? That's the tell-tale sign that you are in a relationship, that you are exclusive.

In our society a kiss is a sign of exclusivity. That's what it means. If you kiss someone, they will expect you to kiss only them and *not* to go around kissing every other person you know. If you kiss someone, don't be surprised when he or she interprets the kiss as a sign of exclusivity. A guy who kisses a girl and is *not* exclusive with her is considered a player, someone not to be trusted. A girl who kisses a guy and turns around and kisses a bunch of other guys is called names I can't even print here. Do not *communicate* exclusivity unless you plan to be exclusive.

Holding Hands

Hand-holding almost always communicates exclusivity (in the United States). You can test this hypothesis on yourself. When you see two of your classmates walking down the hall and holding hands, your first assumption is likely that they are in a relationship.

Parents who want a reading on the seriousness of their

son or daughter's relationship will frequently pay attention to whether hand-holding exists or not. If your parents spot you at the movies with a member of the opposite sex, you can bet they will be trying to catch a glimpse of your hands to see if your fingers are intertwined.

When you want to know whether a member of the opposite sex is available or "taken," you often rely on hand-holding to provide a clue. If Sally "likes" Sam, and one of her friends spots Sam at the movies with another girl, what's Sally's first question? She wants to know, "Were they holding hands?" This fact alone will tell Sally whether Sam is in an exclusive relationship.

From a moral perspective, there is nothing sinful about holding hands. Hand-holding will not cause people to lose their virginity. In fact, hand-holding isn't even particularly arousing. The hands are often sweaty anyway. However, hand-holding is a powerful way of communicating exclusivity in a relationship. Therefore, hand-holding, where there is nothing whatsoever immoral or sexual about it, needs to be reserved for a steady dating relationship specifically because it communicates exclusivity, not just for the evening or the event, but exclusivity with marriage in the back of your mind.

Pretending Touch Doesn't Matter

You can plainly see how physical touch will bond you emotionally to the person you touch. You can see how that's a natural and delightful part of life. Even though this is God's plan, you know as well as I, there are youth who want to get physical just for the fun of it, and they don't care if they are in a relationship or not. This is the "love 'em and leave 'em" type, the type who brag that they didn't even know their partner's name. This is the type who will search for a "make out buddy" simply to gratify their own physical appetites and passions.

You may know those who claim that they can have sex without affection, that they can make out without feeling the need to be in a relationship. They can—eventually. They will have feelings for their partner at first, and the more they work to numb their feelings, the more successful they become at separating physical from emotional intimacy. The ultimate danger of this practice is they actually become numb to the power of touch. It *loses* its ability to bond.

Imagine that I took a piece of duct tape and stuck it on your forearm. Then I yanked it off. What's going to happen? First, that bond that was formed between your arm and my duct tape is going to be broken, and it's going to hurt . . . probably a lot. Now imagine that I took that same duct tape and stuck it on somebody else's arm. What's going to happen? It will hurt a little bit when I rip it off, but it won't hurt nearly as much as the first time, because the duct tape is full of someone else's skin and hair, and it *doesn't stick* like it did the first time. Now imagine I stuck the same strip of duct tape on a third person, and a fourth. Pretty soon, the duct tape will cease to stick at all.

It's possible to have lots of sexual encounters and ignore the fact that these encounters make you want to bond. It's possible that the more you ignore your feelings, the less you feel, and eventually it is possible to have a sexual experience and it's "just sex." It doesn't involve feelings at all.

Should this happen, you can forget ever having a successful marriage. Your ability to bond to a spouse will be wiped out. Research has shown that the greater number of sexual partners you have while dating, the fewer your chances of staying faithful when married.[6]

Even when a woman had only one sexual partner other than her husband during the dating years, her risk of divorce was *three times higher* than for women who had had sex with only their husband.[7]

Clearly emotional intimacy leads to physical intimacy and physical intimacy leads to emotional intimacy. If you control your emotional intimacy, you'll control your physical intimacy. If you control your physical intimacy, you'll also control your emotional intimacy. The goal is to make sure they go together. In whatever stage you want to be, you want to make sure your physical and emotional intimacy match. A good match is absolutely necessary for a successful relationship.

Endnotes

1. John Van Epp, *How to Avoid Falling in Love with a Jerk*, New York: McGraw-Hill, 2008, 288.

2. JeaNette Goates Smith, *Side by Side*, Salt Lake City: Deseret Book, 2004, 27.

3. Juan Mann, accessed May 11, 2012, http://www.freehugscampaign.org/

4. John Van Epp, *How to Avoid Falling in Love with a Jerk*, New York: McGraw-Hill, 2008, 289.

5. Ibid., 291-93.

6. Ibid., 294.

7. Ibid., 295.

Chapter 5

CROSSING the LINES

I RECENTLY HIRED SOME CARPENTERS TO INSTALL cabinets in my kitchen. I was surprised that the first thing they did was turn off all the lights in the kitchen. I wondered how they could install cabinets in the dark. Soon they brought out a tripod with a light on top, which projected a laser beam onto the wall where the cabinets would be installed. When I asked about the red line that appeared on the wall, they explained that that horizontal line helped them keep the cabinets straight. Without it, the cabinets would not be level. I could imagine what would happen if the cabinets were not level when they were installed. I could envision all my glasses sliding to one side of the cabinet, crashing into one another and leaving glass shards all over the countertop. It made a lot of sense that these carpenters wanted a perfectly horizontal line as their guideline so they could get the cabinets installed straight.

Notice that the Funnel Theory has a horizontal line

dividing each stage of a relationship. Within each stage, there are physical behaviors that belong in that stage. The amount of physical intimacy needs to match the amount of emotional intimacy. You could imagine one side of the funnel representing the level of emotional intimacy and the other side of the funnel representing the corresponding level of physical intimacy. Everything falls apart if the line starts to tilt and the emotional stage of a relationship is connected to the wrong physical behavior.

Based on what you have learned in previous chapters, it will be apparent what type of physical intimacy belongs in each stage of a relationship.

STAGE ONE: ACQUAINTANCE

At the beginning of the relationship, when two people first meet (if they live in America), they will shake hands, probably no more, no less. In some countries, people greet with a kiss on the cheek or what I call a "kiss-miss," where they touch cheeks and kiss the air. But in our Western culture we shake hands.

STAGE TWO: FRIENDS

As two people become better friends their level of touch increases as well. They might give one another a high-five or a playful punch in the arm. They may place an arm on top of the other's shoulders or give a brief hug or pat on back.

STAGE THREE: CASUAL DATING

In the casual dating stage, two people are friends who have paired up just for an event, so their interaction will be exactly the same as stage two, friendship. They may be playful, giving one another a brief hug or a kiss on the forehead or the cheek. The physical behavior in this stage is casual—so casual that they could engage in the same physical behavior with all of their friends, and nobody will consider them "loose."

STAGE FOUR: SERIOUS DATING

The physical behaviors that are appropriate in this stage become more intimate specifically because the relationship is exclusive and the couple is old enough to marry. In this stage you do things like hold hands, intertwine fingers, put your arms around one another's waist, or sit on one another's knee. You would most certainly not do the things you do in a serious relationship with anybody and everybody. In a serious, exclusive relationship, it is appropriate to kiss on the lips or give one another a nice long hug.

Just as emotional behavior becomes more intimate as the funnel narrows, physical behavior also gets more intimate. So if there is a level of touch that you wouldn't do with all of your friends, but only with your boyfriend or girlfriend, then you can be pretty sure that touch belongs in the steady dating stage.

STAGE FIVE: ENGAGEMENT

If you choose be exclusive for the rest of eternity, you become engaged. In my opinion, the physical interaction for an engaged couple should be no different than for a couple who are boyfriend and girlfriend. The physical behaviors in a serious dating stage are the same as in the engagement stage. Since you are going to get married, I believe hugging and kissing are appropriate in this stage of the relationship.

Some people believe you should back off on your physical affection once you become engaged because your emotions are so strong that it is really difficult to control your desire to become more and more physical. There are bishops who advise that you never be alone together once you become engaged. It's too easy to rationalize physically intimate behavior with the excuse: "We're getting married anyway. What difference does a few weeks make?"

In general, it is natural to become more physically affectionate with one another, the more emotionally close you get. You do have to exercise self-discipline during the engagement stage so you can stay temple worthy, just like you have to exercise control over your appetites and passions your entire life. You have to "make yourself mind yourself" as someone once said.

STAGE SIX: MARRIAGE

You already know that the type of physical relationship reserved for marriage includes heavy petting, French kissing, and—of course—intercourse. This type of physical interaction is entirely appropriate in a marriage, and marriage is the *only* relationship in which it is appropriate. It doesn't mean that anything goes in a marriage. Just like in all of the other stages, you have to exercise self-discipline and make yourself mind yourself.

A *summary* of the appropriate level of physical intimacy for each stage follows. It is abbreviated for convenience in reading these charts, but is explained above.

Do not show this chart to people unless they have read the previous chapter as well. It won't make sense unless you understand the power of touch.

RULES OF TOUCH*	
acquaintance	handshake
friends	high five
casual dating	brief hug
serious dating	hand-holding/kissing
engagement	kissing
marriage	intercourse

Teens who don't understand the rules of touch can experience a lot of grief. One of the most common ways people hurt one another is by "crossing the lines." Crossing the lines means they are in one stage of a relationship emotionally, yet they introduce the type of touch that belongs in an entirely different stage of the relationship.

Crossing the Lines

An obvious example of crossing the lines, is taking a relationship that is at stage one, acquaintance, (no feelings of affection, no commitment), and mixing it up with the touch belonging in a stage six relationship, marriage. When you have sex with an acquaintance we call it a one-night stand, rape, or date rape. Mixing a stage-one relationship with a stage six level of touch when it's not consensual is a crime.

Another extreme example of crossing the lines is taking a relationship that is at the marriage stage, where there is love and commitment, and mixing it up with the touch that belongs in a stage-one relationship (acquaintance). That would mean that the only touching a married couple would do is to shake hands. How weird is that? That's not a marriage.

STAGE ONE CROSSED WITH STAGE SIX

Stage	Emotional Commitment	Physical Commitment
1	acquaintance	handshake
2	friends	high five
3	casual dating	brief hug
4	serious dating	hold hands/kiss
5	engagement	kissing
6	marriage	intercourse

Most cases of crossing the line are less dramatic than the two just mentioned. However, less dramatic examples of crossing the line can still lead to heartbreak.

Friends with Benefits

Teens commonly cross a stage two relationship (friendship) with a stage five (engagement) level of touch. In other words, two adolescents who are just friends decide to kiss and make out.

STAGE TWO CROSSED WITH STAGE FIVE

Stage	Emotional Commitment	Physical Commitment
1	acquaintance	handshake
2	friends	high five
3	casual dating	brief hug
4	serious dating	hold hands/kiss
5	engagement	kissing
6	marriage	intercourse

Recreational Sex

Others cross a stage-three relationship in which the couple is casually dating with the type of physical intimacy reserved for stage six, marriage. We wouldn't refer to this as prostitution or a one-night stand like we do when a stage-one relationship is crossed with the physical intimacy appropriate in a stage-six relationship. Instead we call it "recreational sex" because the couple who is not even in an exclusive or committed relationship is indulging in the type of physical intimacy appropriate in a stage six relationship.

STAGE THREE CROSSED WITH STAGE SIX

Stage	Emotional Commitment	Physical Commitment
1	acquaintance	handshake
2	friends	high five
3	casual dating	brief hug
4	serious dating	hold hands/kiss
5	engagement	kissing
6	marriage	intercourse

Extreme crossing of the lines occurs quite often in the world. People in stage-one through stage-five relationships want to indulge in the physical behaviors appropriate only in a stage six relationship, marriage. Mere acquaintances or those who are just friends, casually dating, dating steadily, or engaged may want to engage in intercourse.

There are thirty different ways you can cross the lines in a relationship of choice. If you are interested in the other ways, they are described in the appendix of this book.

Skipping Stages

Latter-day Saint youth are more likely to skip a stage than they are to cross the lines. This means you keep the lines parallel, and you match the appropriate level of emotional intimacy with the appropriate level of physical intimacy. You've all been taught not to have sex until marriage, so it's not likely that you will cross any of the emotional stages with the physical behaviors of stage six. But LDS youth have certainly been known to rush into serious relationships (go steady), entirely skipping two very important stages. You can probably guess the stages you are most likely to skip: stages two and three.

Skipping Stage Two

Skipping the friendship stage is the worst thing you can do if you want a compatible relationship. You find out what someone is truly like in the friendship stage. Once you enter a romance stage, you view the relationship with rose-colored glasses. You cannot see the relationship for what it really is because you are clouded by your emotions. A total creep may look like Prince Charming if you love him. Cruella de Vil will look like the virgin Mary when seen through the eyes of her lover. Marriage counselors often give the advice: "Before marriage keep your eyes wide open, and after a marriage, closed tight." This means that you need to overlook one another's faults after you're married. But before you're married—that's the time to see clearly. Stay in the friendship stages long enough to learn what your friend is truly like.

The friendship stage is critical because it will form the foundation of your relationship if it *does* progress into a romance. Couples who have been married for years, and are not currently experiencing fireworks like newlyweds, need to have something solid keeping them together. If they got together simply because they were attracted to one another, and if that attraction wanes, the relationship is in serious trouble. This doesn't mean that attraction goes away after a relationship matures, it means that the attraction isn't as poignant or urgent as it was at the beginning of the romance. This means that something, other than physical urgency, needs to keep a couple together. That something will be a friendship.

One of the foremost researchers on marriage, John Gottman, has found that for a happy marriage, a solid friendship is essential.

The linchpin of a lasting marriage, Gottman finds, is a simple concept with a profound impact: friendship. Successful couples have "a mutual respect for and enjoyment of each other's company." Couples who last "know each other intimately [and] are well versed in each other's likes, dislikes, personality quirks, hopes and dreams. They have an abiding regard for each other and express this fondness" in big and little ways, day in and day out. The quality of their friendship also is the determining factor in whether couples are satisfied with the sex, romance and passion in their marriages.[1]

Rushing into Romance

Lots of kids will skip stages two and three and rush into romance just because it looks so delicious. It reminds me of the dessert menu at a restaurant. I am always tempted by the table tents that greet you as soon as you sit down. There are these luscious pictures of "Chocolate Stampede" or "Death by Chocolate." Many times I have given in to temptation and have just skipped the meal entirely and ordered dessert instead. It tastes really good while I'm eating it, but I always have a stomachache later. And what's worse, I'm still hungry.

Teens may choose to skip friendship and casual dating and rush right into steady dating for many reasons. One reason is other people in your life are so excited for you to have a one-and-only that they push you into a serious relationship. When I was in high school, I spent a lot of time in the home of my best friend. Whenever I would walk in the door, the first thing her mother would say after "Hi" is "How's David?" or whomever I had gone out with most recently. Then she would continue to quiz me: "You guys an item?" "Is he the one?" I always felt as if I was disappointing her when I didn't have anything to report. Her face fell, and she left the room when she discovered that there was no news.

A second reason young people rush into steady dating and skip the casual dating stage is jealousy. Yep. Just like in junior high. You get insecure when your friend has another friend besides you, so you do everything you can to keep him or her all to yourself.

I know a young lady (I'll call her Martha) who was asked out on a casual date by Kurt (not his real name). They went to a concert and had a lot of fun together, and Martha wanted Kurt to ask her out again. He probably would have too, except she got so jealous when he took out Kimberly the next weekend that she wouldn't even talk to him. After one single date, Martha expected him to be faithful to her, as if a single date a match makes. When Kurt didn't meet her expectation, she totally wrote him off.

I've seen a young man and a young lady go on a casual date together and have so much fun that the young man asked the young lady out again the next weekend. However, she already had plans to go out with someone else. He was crushed. He thought he did something wrong. He thought she didn't like him. He vowed to never ask her out again. This is tragic. A couple never really has the chance to get to know one another at their leisure when their casual dates are expected to immediately become serious.

There are all kinds of reasons kids are tempted to skip friendship and casual dating. Some youth rush into romance because they are insecure; some have a problematic home life. But rushing romance is not worth it. You have too much to lose. Friendship and casual dating are the exact two stages of a relationship you guys should be enjoying at this time of your lives. President Hinckley counseled:

> When you are young, do not get involved in steady dating. When you reach an age where you think of marriage, then is the time to become so involved. But you boys who are in high school don't need this, and neither do the girls.
>
> We receive letters, we constantly deal with people who, under the pressures of life, marry while very young. There is an old saying, "Marry in haste, repent at leisure." How true that is.
>
> Have a wonderful time with the young women. Do things together but do not get too serious too soon. You have missions ahead of you, and you cannot afford to compromise this great opportunity and responsibility.[2]

Spending time in the friendship and casual dating stages does not mean you won't eventually make it to the steady dating stage. You will still progress from one stage to another. In time, friends may become lovers, and lovers may marry. But you can't be in such a hurry to get to the steady dating stage that you compromise those very relationships you were so eager to have. You will experience more joy and more success in your romantic relationships if you take your time in the preceding stages.

Endnotes

1. John Gottman as cited in Karen S. Peterson, "Friendship Makes Marriages a Success," *USA Today*, April 1, 1999.

2. Gordon B. Hinckley, "A Prophet's Counsel and Prayer for Youth," *Ensign*, Nov. 1997.

Chapter 6

Emotional Dangers of Rushing Romance

MANY YOUTH THINK THE BIGGEST DANGER OF rushing into an emotionally intimate relationship in high school is physical intimacy. Those of you who think physical intimacy is the only danger of emotional intimacy may rationalize your serious relationships, claiming, "We are strong. We can handle it. We won't give in to temptation."

Of course this is naïve, and you won't even realize it until it's too late. Even if you did happen to have the discipline of Edward Cullen, there are plenty of other reasons to avoid emotionally intimate relationships in high school. Emotionally intimate relationships all by themselves, even if they don't become too physically intimate, will cause you heartache.

I am a marriage and family therapist by vocation. That means I get to spend my days listening to couples tell me all about their relationships. After twenty years of doing this, I am thoroughly convinced that two things contribute to bad relationships that we can totally eliminate: (1) marrying without shopping around and (2) traumatic high school relationships.

When you get too serious too soon, you may marry too soon, without searching hard enough to find the right person. Then you're stuck in the marriage and end up visiting a therapist like me, who is supposed to fix a relationship that shouldn't have been in the first place. High school is the time to do your homework . . . and I don't mean math and English. I mean do your relationship homework. Find out what's out there before you jump to the conclusion you've found your true love.

Shop Around

The magazine *CosmoGirl* ran an article called "Four Guys to Date before You Graduate." The article claims, "Guys are like electives: You've got to take a bunch before you decide to commit to a major!" The article encourages girls not to "love 'em and leave 'em," but to have fun spending time with new guys. "If you lock yourself into a specific type too soon, you'll miss out on the great unknown of what might be better for you."[1]

You will get along with some people better than others. You are not going to be compatible with everybody, even if you come from the same religious background. Teenage years are the time to do your homework and find out whom you're compatible with. It's not time to take the final exam.

President David O. McKay taught the importance of avoiding serious relationships in high school:

> Associations are conducive to happy marriages because young folks become acquainted with

one another and have more opportunity of choice . . . Going steady limits, if not excludes, girls and boys from having the opportunity of becoming acquainted with one another . . . Ever be mindful that following childhood, youth has other obligations besides choosing a mate . . . Going steady may so enchant the couple that these other associated obligations may be given too little consideration.[2]

If you don't take a few electives, you may end up with a major you really don't like. Being friends with lots of members of the opposite sex can help you discover what type of person you get along with. You may discover you like a planner, the kind of person who schedules dates in advance and is always on time, or you may like a more spontaneous person, who is game for anything with a moment's warning. You may discover you like a talkative individual, with whom you can have a stimulating conversation for hours at a time, or you might like a quiet individual, with whom you can sit comfortably in silence. You may discover you like a person who has strong family ties, who visits and communicates frequently with his family, or you may like a person who is more independent and lives away from his family. You may like an active person who rises early, crams all kinds of activities into a day, and never seems to slow down, or you may like a more laid-back person who is happy staying home and limiting social contacts. You won't know what type of person you get along with the best unless you casually date a variety of people.

You learn things when you casually date lots of different people that you can't learn if you lock yourself into one relationship too early:

- Male-female differences
- What type of person is trustworthy
- How you/others deserve to be treated
- The basis of relationships is friendship
- How people handle money
- How people treat their parents
- What you see is not what you get
- Love is not enough
- How religion affects behavior
- The value of honesty

When I was in college, my best friend lined me up with her cousin. He was pretty cute, and I trusted her opinion, so I went out with him with my hopes high. We had dated for several weeks when I discovered he wasn't planning to finish college. I knew he had dropped out for a semester to sell real estate, but I always thought he was going to return to get his degree. When he told me he never planned to return to college, I couldn't hide my alarm.

Before I could put my hand over my mouth, I burst out, "What? You don't want a college degree?" He could see I was disappointed, and I tried to take back my words. "Oh, that's okay. Lots of people make good livings without a college degree." But he knew. We both knew. I valued education more than he did, and it would always be difficult for me to admire him the way he wanted to be admired. We decided to end the relationship.

You need experience with a variety of casual relationships. You need to see that love doesn't make the world go round, that loving relationships don't necessarily mean lasting relationships. You need to recognize that people are usually on their best behavior when trying to impress a significant other, and that behavior may be completely different when the significant other is out of sight.

Learning about Yourself

Dating a variety of people without getting serious allows you to determine what type of person you like, and it also helps you determine what types of things you like.

Chumming up with different people allows you to discover where your talents lie. You will discover what things interest you and what you are good at. One friend may introduce you to music or dance or theater, and you may discover you have a passion for the arts. Another friend may introduce you to the outdoors, and you develop an interest in hiking, climbing, or biking. Another friend may introduce you to history or literature, and you discover that these subjects are fulfilling. Most people discover their passions through personal associations—a friend invites you to come and try some new activity.

My son Spencer invited his friend Mike to come wakeboarding with us one summer. Spencer was a pretty good wakeboarder and taught Mike to get up and cut and jump the wake. Pretty soon they were doing Supermans, flips, and air-raleys together. Before we knew it, Mike won a bunch of contests, got a sponsor, and went pro! He learned about what he liked from his friendships.

Another son became friends with Snow White while he was in college. Seriously. This young lady worked at Disneyland and dressed up like Snow White and signed autographs for children from all over the world. My son learned all about the bodyguards that surrounded her and the foreign tourists' passion for American folk heroes. After befriending Snow White, he actually considered working for a cruise line and playing Hercules as part of their on-board entertainment. Another dream eventually won out over this one; however, he became a more well-rounded and interesting person because of this friendship.

Jayne B. Malan says in her essay "The Summer of the Lambs" that "adolescence is your time to grow physically, mentally, socially, and spiritually. This is the time to study hard in school and to learn more about the gospel along with ways to live and share it. It's the time to take advantage of every opportunity that comes along to develop your talents and make friends—lots of friends."

Would you go into Nordstrom and buy the first pair of shoes you tried on? If you did, they might cause lots of blisters before you wore them in. Wise shoppers will try on a few pair of shoes to make sure they are buying the one with the best fit. While blisters do heal and become callouses, your marriage will be much easier if you marry the right person in the first place.

Too Much of What You Don't Need

Rushing into romance not only deprives you of what you absolutely *need*, it also exposes you to what you definitely *don't need*. It is alarming enough to learn that youth who pair up in high school miss out on social experiences they desperately need to create a great marriage. Equally alarming is the fact that if you go steady in high school, you experience some trauma that can damage you emotionally. Then it becomes difficult to have a good relationship even when you do find the right partner.

Have you noticed all the drama that surrounds teenage

romance? Couples who go steady are constantly fighting, hurting one another, breaking up, and making up. It seems the more serious the relationship gets, the greater the drama.

Did you ever wonder why all the drama? Why can't teenagers in romantic relationships just get along like in the movies? Why can't the relationship simply be full of starry nights and fragrant roses?

You will figure out why teenagers constantly fight when you pay attention to what they fight about. They fight about fidelity: "I saw you talking to that other guy in the lunch line. He was flirting with you." They fight about the time they spend together: "You're always playing ball with your friends and never spend any time with me." They fight about how far they should go physically: Generally, he's frustrated because she keeps telling him telling him "no."

In an effort to "have their cake and eat it too," teenagers may want to be in a monogamous relationship, but they also want to "play the field." They want a monogamous relationship because of advantages it provides: security, convenience, reassurance, and so on. On the other hand, they do not want a monogamous relationship because of all the restrictions it provides: the need to be accountable for one's whereabouts, companions, and activities, and the limitations on whom one can see, spend time with, and associate with. Therefore, the high school romantic is highly motivated to appear faithful while still pursuing other interests. Is it any wonder that adolescent relationships are filled with deception and mistrust?

No matter how good you are together, no matter how much your relationship is "meant to be," any couple that tries to get too serious too soon is going to have problems. A relationship that might have a chance in five years is ruined because you indulged too soon. It's like taking a cake out of the oven before it's done baking and trying to cut a slice. It's a gooey mess. If you are patient and wait until the buzzer goes off and the cake cools, it will be delicious.

You're supposed to talk to other kids in the lunch line. It's way too soon to settle down with one person. Of course you're going to spend time with your other friends. You need more than one friend.

The Trauma of Drama

It's hard to imagine that an adolescent would be dumb enough to place his or her trust in someone who has no motive to be faithful and every motive to be unfaithful. The truth is, adolescents aren't that dumb. That's why they are so suspicious. Adolescents seem to know that there is a good chance their romantic relationships will end. It is only a question of when.

The expectation of deceit can create all kinds of trust issues in adolescent relationships. The most tragic result of trusting the untrustworthy is that this experiment can actually damage your ability to love with all your heart.

The danger occurs when repeated attempts to find loyal love all end the same way: with disloyalty. Teens who repeatedly enter into relationships in which they are going to be "dropped" or taken for granted eventually become untrusting. They enter relationships expecting to be hurt and may even create situations where they are bound to be hurt, just to prove they are right.

Teenagers who have been through this kind of hurt may refuse to trust even when they are old enough to sustain a relationship and happen upon a trustworthy mate. They are convinced that opening up to another individual results in being hurt, so they are extremely reluctant, and in some cases, unable, to open up.

Horrible relationship lessons can severely impact your chance for a happy marriage. If you settle for a relationship based on mutual using, you will expect to be hurt and will refuse to open up and become vulnerable. Relationships that could have succeeded end up failing because of insecurities and paranoia. Baggage from adolescence affects the adult relationship.

Don't you wonder if our nation's 50-percent-plus divorce rate would be lower if people didn't engage in so many careless romances before marriage? I do not think it is a stretch at all to say that if youth would postpone their romantic relationships until they are at least out of high school, we could significantly reduce the nation's divorce rate.

Not Meant to Be

Teens who get too serious cannot treat one another as well as a child of God deserves to be treated. Even if they want to be everything to one another, they don't have the ability. You may want to give one another a brand-new convertible, but you don't have the ability.

There is a powerful story about two young people who emigrate from Ireland just before the turn of the century. They are not a couple, but the girl, who is wealthy, offers to pay the way for the boy, who is poor, because she is running away from home and cannot travel alone. They live together in a rented room, pretending to be brother and sister. As you might expect—sharing one another's lives, living in close proximity, and experiencing several crises together—they fall in love. However, by this time, they have been robbed of all their earthly possessions, they become homeless, and ultimately the girl gets shot. The boy knows the girl's parents have come to America to look for her, but the last thing he wants is to return her to her parents because they will keep her from ever seeing him again. Nevertheless, he is in absolutely no position to take care of her. He has no money, no job, no home, and is unable to pay a doctor to remove the bullet. As much as the boy wants to take care of her, he simply can't. He doesn't have the ability. He carries her bleeding and near death, and leaves her with her family who is in a position to take care of her.[3]

As grown-up as you look, and as grown-up as you may feel, you still possess characteristics you will grow out of when you become adults. Teenagers simply aren't in a position to take care of a romantic partner the way they deserve.

Experts who study adolescent behavior have identified the following characteristics that interfere with intimate relationships. Teens generally

- are inherently self-centered
- have a sense of invulnerability (which means they don't yet understand that what goes around comes around)
- are poor decision-makers and are often impulsive
- believe love comes in a fixed amount (which means they will create conflict with a parent in order to be intimate with a boyfriend or girlfriend)
- are idealistic (they have no patience for the realities of an intimate relationship)

- have a tenuous identity (they can be easily influenced by a significant other)[4]

Further research, reported by Charlene Kemper of the Dibble Institute at a Smart Marriages Conference in 2010, revealed that adolescents

- overreact to minor situations

- experience wide mood swings

Do you want to be in an exclusive relationship with someone possessing these qualities? This helps you understand why 30 percent of the teenagers who are going steady experience dating violence.[5] Teenagers lack the emotional maturity to be in a healthy romantic relationship.

Guys won't possess these negative characteristics to such a great extent when they become young adults. Neither will girls. You grow out of them. Literally. Your brain is the last organ to stop growing in your body. When it finishes forming, you think differently.

No wonder so many teenage romances are plagued with drama. Teenagers aren't wired to exercise the selflessness or the patience required in an exclusive relationship. Going steady in high school is like Cinderella's stepsister trying to shove her foot into the glass slipper. It's not a fit. You can force it, but either the slipper or the foot will break.

Endnotes

1. Jessica Blatt, "4 Guys to Date Before You Graduate," *CosmoGirl*, Nov. 2004, 117.

2. David O. McKay, "Youth of a Noble Birthright [1960]," as quoted in *Achieving a Celestial Marriage Instructor's Guide*, Salt Lake City, UT: CES Department of

Seminaries and Institutes of Religion, 1976, 141.

3. *Far and Away*, 1992.

4. David Elkind, *All Grown Up and No Place to Go*, Boston: Da Capo Press, 1998, 34-39.

5. "50 Things Everyone Should Know about Dating Violence," pamphlet, Santa Cruz, CA: Journeyworks Publishing, 2004.

Chapter 7

Better Than Romance

YOU PROBABLY SAW THE TITLE OF THIS CHAPTER AND thought to yourself, "What could possibly be better than romance?" Well, in the grand scheme of things, not much. However, while you're in high school, friendship is far better than romance.

Expanding Your Horizons

Friendship among adolescents is, frankly, more enriching. You get to participate in more activities, meet more people, and learn more about the world. You become more well-rounded and better educated when you are not *stuck* in one steady relationship.

I benefited so much from the friendships I developed with young men when I was in high school. One young man taught me how to write news articles, which I later did as a part-time job. Another taught me about photography, which allowed me to illustrate my news articles and get paid a bit more for them. It took three different guys to teach me to drive a clutch: one with a Toyota Celica, one in a Datsun Z car, and one with a Bronco (the hardest clutch I ever drove—I rolled backward on a hill into the car behind us!). Some of the young men were the adventurous type: one took me touring in a glider, another took me tandem on a hang glider, I was talked into my first mud-bath by another, and another persuaded me to start a business sewing baggy pants he had seen worn in Taiwan. Thank goodness for the brainiacs: one who was an expert on world religions taught me the history and relationship between Muslims, Buddhists, Hindus, Christians, and Jews; while another helped me pass calculus.

I had never been involved in athletics until I started casually dating.

Before I knew it, I had met a guy who tried to teach me to play tennis—I was terrible at first. Several guys took me water skiing—it became my favorite sport. Another took me hiking—which I also came to love. Another taught me that fights were expected in hockey games, and grabbed me before I ran to notify the police. One marvelous man taught me the difference between a touchdown and a first down, and he also taught me how to snow ski (I married him).

My world is so much richer, and I am a more well-rounded person because I had such a wide variety of friends during my high school years.

I previously mentioned an article I was lured into reading entitled, "4 Guys to Date Before You Graduate" and the subtitle was, "Guys are like electives: You've got to take a bunch before you decide to commit to a major!"[1] It doesn't really matter what four types of guys the magazine recommend these girls date; what matters is that they clearly recognized it is not wise for girls to get tied down to one guy too soon.

If you lock yourself into a specific type too soon, you'll miss out on the great unknown of what might be better for you.

We're not saying you should use these guys and then drop them! But you'll have *fun* spending time with new guys. And you'll realize how interesting it is to expand your horizons and really learn about guys, [friendships,] and yourself.

Be Yourself

In a friendship, as opposed to a romance, you can be yourself. You don't have to impress your friends. They know all about you and love you just the same.

I knew a girl in high school who didn't think it was ladylike to have a healthy appetite. Before each date, she would eat a hearty meal and then at the restaurant she would pick at her food. I always wondered what would happen if any of her relationships progressed to marriage. What would her spouse think when he suddenly discovered that she actually liked to eat?

Friends accept each other just the way they are; you don't feel the need to "fake good" just to keep a friend. Friends don't need to hide their past, their family secrets, or their bad habits. They may even disclose family trauma in an effort to derive comfort from their friends.

When you can be yourself and your friends still accept you, it feels a lot better than the knowledge that you are being accepted because they like someone you are pretending to be.

So many fairy tales depict characters who are not being

themselves, and they are trying to deceive the person they have fallen in love with. Mulan pretends to be a man, which is really inconvenient when she falls in love with her general, Li Shang. Jasmine, the daughter of the king, pretends to be a pauper so that Aladdin, the poor street rat, won't be intimidated by her, while Aladdin pretends to be a rich prince, so Jasmine will notice and love him. Ariel, the mermaid, actually makes a deal with Ursula, the sea witch, by which she will temporarily become human so she can catch her man. What would have happened if this didn't end happily ever after, and she turned back into a mermaid after Eric married her?

Friendships trump romance during adolescence because friendship is easier than romance—it's far less stressful. Girls are less threatening to boys when they can just be friends. The boys don't get dry mouth when talking on the phone, or sweaty palms before knocking on the door. The boys don't worry about impressing the girls. If the friendship works, great. If it doesn't, there will be others. The same is true of girls who believe in friendship. It is far less nerve-wracking to spend time with boys if you're not terrified of disappointing them.

More Fun

My husband had a friend when he was in high school who was undoubtedly the most popular girl in the school. She was invited to every prom, every homecoming, and every social, because she didn't have a boyfriend. She was the one girl in the school who didn't believe in going steady, so she was never "taken," and nobody had to worry about offending her boyfriend.

Whenever a school dance came around, and inevitably

some guy wouldn't have a date, this girl was the go-to girl. She got to fly to prom in a helicopter; ride on a steam train; and eat dinner on an overpass, in the back of a U-Haul, and on a freeway median. Every time there was a big group date being planned and all the guys had to find a date, the young lady without a steady boyfriend was the logical choice. She went out with all kinds of different guys, didn't get serious with any of them, and never lacked for fun.

One young lady shares her view of friendship dating:

I don't know about you, but I love to flirt. I love to flirt with a lot of different people; often times the boy at the ticket window of the movie theater, or a waiter at a restaurant. (A little discount never hurts, right?) Because I am not seriously dating anyone, I am in no way labeled a cheater. I have the right to flirt with variety of people. There is so much freedom in being single. Whenever "Riding Solo" by Jason Derulo comes on the radio, I blast it. "I feel like a star, I can't stop my shining." This is how I feel being single as a youth. I am not tied down.

Friends for Life

When you build your relationship on a foundation of friendship, you'll get a pretty good idea whether a romance would succeed. If you determine it would never succeed then you can remain friends. This is really wise if you plan to settle down in the same town where you did your courting. You don't have to endure the embarrassment of getting the whole town excited about your romance, only to watch it break up later. You don't have to experience the weirdness of bumping into your ex everywhere you go. You can continue to associate with the same group of friends without your spouse being threatened by your ex.

Let me warn you how totally awkward it is to live in the same town as your ex. It's even worse if you happen to live in the same ward as your ex. One of the couples I see in marriage counseling is having trouble precisely because the husband's ex is in their ward, and the wife can't curb her jealousy. If you don't want to move clear across the country, be careful that you don't get serious with someone who will clearly never become your spouse.

Too often, members of the same ward start to date seriously while in high school, and when they break up one of them stops coming to church. It is just too awkward for them to bump into their ex every Sunday morning. This happens especially often where I live and there are a lot of young converts to the church. These converts are sometimes shaky at the beginning anyway, and if they experience an adolescent romance gone wrong, they are not strong enough to stay active.

I was a member of the seminary council when I was in high school. This was like the governing body of the seminary. Since I grew up in Salt Lake City, half of the student body attended seminary. There was a strict rule for members of the seminary council: no pairing off. We were not allowed to seriously date anyone else on the council. We were required to remain just friends—otherwise we could not serve on the council. This rule existed because too many council members had gotten serious with one another, and then when they broke up they couldn't stand to be in the same room with one another, so it affected their ability to serve in their position on the council.

The young men with whom I served on this seminary council became some of the dearest friends of my high school career. Because we knew we could not date seriously, the relationships were casual, relaxed, not pressured, open, and fun. We could tease one another and joke together, and we never had to worry about impressing one another. As we grew older, we stayed in touch, we all found people to marry, and we still remained friends with one another. One of my friends from seminary moved across the country to where my husband and I were living. He and his wife became our houseguests while they were looking for a place of their own. His wife and I became pool partners and together took our children swimming in the summer.

Another friend from the council became a dentist and performed beautiful work on my teeth and later those of my siblings, their spouses, and their children (I trusted his professional skills because I had seen what a perfectionist he was during our friendship). I never had to "break up" with any of these guys because we never were an "item." Our friendships have been mutually rewarding for decades, something that would have been nearly impossible had we had a romantic relationship.

Better at Choosing a Marriage Partner

Youth who have a wide variety of friends, rather than restricting themselves to a single relationship, will be better informed when the time comes to choose a marriage partner.

In an evening of pleasurable dancing and conversation, one can become acquainted with many splendid young folk, every one of whom has admirable traits and may be superior to any one companion in at least some qualities. Here partners can begin to appraise and evaluate, noting qualities, attainments and superiorities by comparison and contrast. Such perceptive friendships can be the basis for wise, selective, occasional dating for those of sufficient age and maturity, this to be followed later in proper timing by steady dating, and later by proper courtship which culminates in a happy, never-ending marriage.[2]

President Kimball is suggesting you appraise and evaluate members of the opposite sex while in the friendship stage in order to determine whom you will, in the proper time, steadily date, and later marry.

The author of the book *Dateworthy* says, "The more people you date, the easier it is to keep from getting too involved too soon with the wrong person. . . . Anyone who expects you to commit in the early stages of dating is a red-flag personality."[3]

As a youth, you must not let anybody persuade you to become exclusive when you are still doing your homework in the friendship stage.

Robert K. McIntosh, an institute director in California, said,

"One of the major purposes of dating ['casual dating' I might add] is to get to know other people. As you do this you will also get to know yourself. Through dating you will learn to identify the qualities and characteristics you desire in an eternal companion."[4]

Better at Being Married

Friendship rocks for yet another reason. Not only do high school friendships help you better choose a marriage partner, they also help you *be* a better marriage partner when the time comes. When you learn to be a friend, you learn to communicate honestly. You learn to make some personal sacrifices. You may learn independence. You learn dependability. You may learn to be decisive. The very traits that drive your friends nuts will also drive your eventual spouse nuts. If you learn, while in a friendship, which traits work and which don't work, you learn not to carry the ones that don't work into a marriage.

Some argue that all those bad romances adolescents endure help them have better relationships as adults. Quite the opposite is the case.

> Children are today exposed to every nuance of human vice and depravity under the mistaken assumption that this will somehow inure them to evil and prepare them to live successful, if not virtuous and honorable, lives. This assumption rests on the mistaken belief that a bad experience is the best preparation for a bad experience. In fact, just the reverse is true: *a good experience is the best preparation for a bad experience.* [5]

This statement is particularly true with relationships. You don't have to experience dysfunction to know how to have a functional relationship. Dysfunctional adolescent relationships put you at greater risk of having dysfunctional adult relationships. Functional, healthy adolescent relationships are the best preparation for healthy, unscarred adult relationships.

Endnotes

1. Jessica Blatt, "4 Guys to Date Before You Graduate," *CosmoGirl*, Nov. 2004, 117.

2. Spencer W. Kimball, *The Miracle of Forgiveness*, Salt Lake City, UT: Deseret Book, 1969, 221-22.

3. Dennie Hughes, "Dennie's 8 Simple Rules for Dating," *USA Weekend*, Feb. 13, 2005.

4. Robert McIntosh, *How Do You Know When You're Really In Love?*, Salt Lake City, UT: Deseret Book, 2000, 125.

5. David Elkind, *All Grown Up and No Place to Go*, Boston: Da Capo Press, 1998, 100. Emphasis added.

Chapter 8

FiRSt COMeS FRieNdShiP

YOU HAVE HEARD THE DITTY CHILDREN OFTEN SING when they see a boy and a girl playing together:

"Two little lovers, sitting in a tree,
k-i-s-s-i-n-g
First comes love,
Then comes marriage,
Then comes baby
In a baby carriage"

A young boy sits next to a girl on the bus, and the chanting begins. A boy picks a girl for his kickball team, and the chanting begins. The young boy and the young girl are caught playing a game of jacks in the driveway, and the chanting begins.

"Moooooom, they're teasing me," the victim of such a chant might complain. The poor child has simply found a playmate, and the singers automatically assume the relationship is about love and marriage.

How incredibly amazing that of all the people you'll meet in your life, you will only marry one of them, yet when children see a boy and a girl together, they jump to the conclusion that the relationship is that one.

Friendship as the Ultimate Goal

Not all of your relationships make it all the way down the funnel. The vast majority of them never make it past friendship. You'll only marry one person in your lifetime (hopefully). You'll only be engaged to one person (hopefully). You'll only go steady with a few people. All the other relationships you have will be acquaintances or friendships.

Even the relationship that eventually does become a romance, *must* have a solid foundation of friendship. Therefore, in high school it's sensible to treat your all your relationships as friendships.

Admittedly, it's hard to remain friends if you are attracted to one another. Sometimes you have the best intentions, but you still keep crushing on this guy or girl. You want to stay friends, but you *like* him or her so much.

Secrets to Staying Friends

The secret to maintaining healthy friendships in high school, without rushing into romance, is to *plan* on the relationship not making it past friendship. Interact as if friends is *all you'll ever be.*

It's tempting to rush into romance if you see romance as a *possibility.* When you stop imagining whether this relationship could someday become a romance, it will be far easier to remain friends.

If things change in years to come, when you are in a position to marry, it will never hurt that you had a fabulous friendship first, without a hint of romance. For now, put the possibility of "someday" completely out of your mind.

One young lady shares the following experience:

I grew up with Joey, a boy who lives down the street from me. I am three days older than he is, and our moms used to trade babysitting. We were hanging out together when we were two, and have been hanging out together ever since. We walked to the bus stop together. We were in the same class in kindergarten, first, second, and third grade. When we finally got put in different classes in fourth grade, Joey cried. When we entered high school, we drove together. Our friends always said, "You guys should go together. You make such a cute couple." Joey and I knew we would never be a couple. He was a die-hard Catholic, and I a committed Latter-day Saint. Because we knew we would never, ever end up together, it made it really easy to stay friends.

Dating as Friends

Sometimes my audiences call casual dating "friendship dating" or "going out as friends." I really like the term "friendship dating," and if you guys want to use that term instead of casual dating, go for it. I think it reminds you that you are in a friendship and not to expect romance.

Just like you used to go on daddy-daughter dates, and it didn't mean you were in a romantic relationship with your dad (eeewwww), you can go out on dates with a member of the opposite sex, which doesn't mean you are in a romantic relationship. Gong on a date with your friend can be loads of fun.

In a survey taken by *USA Weekend*, thirty-seven thousand students responded to the question, "Which of these scenarios would you most enjoy for a Saturday night?

1. Hanging out with a *group* of guys and girls, or
2. Hanging out with someone with whom you are romantically interested

More than twice as many respondents (49 percent of guys and 64 percent of girls) preferred hanging out with a group over hanging out with a romantic partner (28 percent of guys and 19 percent of girls).

Finding Friends

Teens have a completely different priority list when looking for a friend then when looking for a boyfriend or girlfriend. When I speak to a small group, I like to quiz them to see what they look for in a friend, versus a boyfriend or girlfriend. It's so amazing to see the difference.

This is what the chart usually looks like:

WHAT BOYS LOOK FOR	
in a friend	in a girlfriend
1. nice	1. hot
2. fun	2. popular
3. easy to talk to	3. not stuck-up

WHAT GIRLS LOOK FOR	
in a friend	in a boyfriend
1. fun	1. good-looking
2. loyal	2. nice car
3. similar values	3. athletic

Looks aren't even an issue when you're looking for a friend but suddenly become paramount when considering a boyfriend/girlfriend. This may be nature's way of perpetuating a handsome species, for those who eventually marry. But when you are just friends, what difference does it make if your friends have thick hair or smooth skin?

Therefore, if you truly want a friendship and not a romance, don't worry about looks. Choose your friends based on their character, not their appearance. The hidden advantage of this method is that you won't be tempted to be romantic with a friend because you simply aren't attracted to your friend.

My daughter claims it's easy for her to see boys as friends and not boyfriends because she just compares them to her brothers and knows exactly how to behave. "My brothers love competition," she says. "They race to see who gets the front seat in the car. They compete to see who can fit the most number of grapes in his mouth. They time each other to see who can hold his breath under water the longest. They race on the ski slopes. They arm wrestle. They compare who can jump the highest over the wake. I learned that boys love to compete. So when I'm with a guy, I treat him like my brothers. 'Bet you can't walk on your hands,' I'll challenge them. They always want to take me on. We end up having so much fun. It makes a big difference that I grew up with boys because I learned what they like to do *besides* make out."

Honesty, Honesty, Honesty

You just learned the secret to staying friends without becoming romantic. Let me share the secret to staying friends without becoming enemies: *Don't play games*. Don't pretend you're totally into the guy or girl you're with if you're not. Don't hide the fact that you go out with other guys/girls. Your same-gender friendships would never succeed if you started lying to your buddies. Your opposite-gender friendships won't succeed either unless you are honest.

BE HONEST ABOUT THE NATURE OF YOUR RELATIONSHIP

Before you ever hop in the car with your date, you should both know what to expect from the date. You should plainly state at the outset that you are not interested in having a boyfriend/girlfriend. Make sure you are both aware that this is a casual date.

You can blame the adults if you need to . . . I always tell my kids that I'm willing to be the fall guy. If you don't have the courage to say, "I choose not to go steady," you can always say, "My parents won't let me go steady." The hope is that, as you become more confident, you can take responsibility for your choices, but if you need a crutch in the meantime, that's what parents are for.

One really easy way to communicate that you want to go on a friendship date is to ask, "Who else is coming?" The moment a guy calls and asks if a girl is available, the girl should let him know she expects others to come along.

Guys can save a girl this trouble if they let her know from the start, "John and Sarah and I are going to the movies tomorrow, do you want to come?

A guy might say, "We should go to the movies

tomorrow. Who else do you want to invite?" At the very same time you are making plans to do something together, make plans to include others.

BE HONEST ABOUT YOUR AFFECTION

Just because you don't want to go steady doesn't mean you don't seriously value your friendships. Make this clear as glass. Say it in a way that can't be misunderstood.

"I had so much fun with you tonight. We really should do this again."

"You really are great company. You know just how to make me laugh."

One of the reasons teenagers are tempted to "go steady" is that it provides them some reassurance that their friend really likes them.

Do you remember back in junior high when you'd pass notes in the lunchroom: "Will you go with me?" You never intended to go anywhere. It was just a way to be reassured that this person liked you. The person was willing to let you tell everybody you were in a relationship.

It should not be necessary to announce to the world that you are together in order to receive reassurance that you are liked. You can like lots of people. You don't have to choose just one. In junior high you may have felt the need to be the "favorite" or the one-and-only. However, as you grow up you realize you can still be liked without being the only one that's liked. You can like someone without "going" with them.

Reassure your friends that you like them, even though you won't go steady with them.

BE HONEST ABOUT YOUR OTHER RELATIONSHIPS

Once a parent from Texas came up to me after a

presentation and claimed that his daughters had been doing just what I had said—doing their "homework," going out with lots of guys, not getting serious with any of them—and they had been labeled sluts. Gasp. I was horrified. That's exactly the opposite of what we want to happen. What could have gone wrong?

I spoke with this dad at length, and I discovered exactly what had ruined his daughters' attempts to casually date—secrets. The girls had been deceiving each and every boy they went out with, making him think he was the one-and-only. They weren't being physical with any of the guys. They were simply hiding the fact that they were going out with other guys too. It made the guys feel stupid, like they were being led on.

Although neither of these girls had actually been physical with any of the boys they were dating and they weren't serious with any of them, the fact that the girls were so secretive about the other relationships made the guys feel like those other relationships must be serious. If those relationships were truly friendships, there was no reason to hide them.

The boys jumped to the conclusion that they were each a one-and-only one simply because the girls had neglected to tell them that they weren't. The girls didn't lie; they just didn't tell the whole truth. The boys retaliated by spreading nasty rumors about the girls.

Overcommunicating

I often tell my clients it's better to overcommunicate than to under-communicate. You may be a little bit annoying when you say to your ride, "Remember we're leaving at eight o'clock—we need to be on time." And then again, "Don't forget, we can't be late. Be sure to be here at eight." But being slightly annoying will prevent lots of anger if your ride shows up at eight thirty and you entirely miss your event.

You can overcommunicate and avoid being annoying if you are skilled at soliciting feedback. If you say, "Can you be here at eight?" and you get a response, "I think so. Nobody else is using the car that evening." You can be pretty certain you were heard. If you say, "Be sure to be here at eight" and you don't get a response, you can't always guarantee you were heard. If you don't want to repeat yourself, ask for feedback.

In the case of casual dating, you might say, "I went to a hockey game with Trent last Saturday. Do you like hockey"? Or you might say, "David asked me to come watch him wrestle on Saturday. What do you think about wrestling?"

When you are on a friendship date and another friend texts you, don't hide your phone, and say, "Oh, it was nobody." Tell your date: "Oh, that was Sean. He wants to go to the fair this weekend. You should come." If Sean is threatened because you invited somebody else to the fair, then go back to the first two rules of honesty: (1) Be honest about the nature of your relationship, and (2) Be honest about your affection.

"Just Friends"

Talk about turning a good word into a bad one. Have you noticed that people who use the name of the Lord in vain, or use the name of Jesus Christ in vain can take a perfectly wonderful name and give it a negative connotation?

The same thing has happened to the term "just friends." Rather than feeling flattered when someone wants to be "just friends" you are likely to feel insulted. This is because teens frequently use the term "just friends" when they want to break up. In order to let one another down gently, teens end a romantic relationship by suggesting they become "just friends." Therefore, you too often see friendship as a consolation prize. The phrase "we're just friends" implies the relationship has a lesser status than a relationship that is "more than friends."

In reality, friendship should never be considered a consolation prize for a romance that didn't work out. Friendship between young men and young women is an honor and can benefit you both.

Chapter 9

NO Such Thing as Falling in Love

IMAGINE YOURSELF STANDING IN THE MOONLIGHT, FACE to face with the man of your dreams, staring into his eyes and he whispers in your ear, "I've decided to love you."

What? Stop the music. How romantic is that? You want him to say, "I'm head-over-heels, hopelessly, helplessly in love with you." Now that's romance—the out-of-control, heart-comes-before-the-head, "I can't survive without you" kind of romance. You can be certain true love exists when there's no way for him to avoid his feelings, can't you?

Actually, no. As flattering as it might feel to have somebody become helpless on your account, to have all reason leave their brain because of your charm is not what love is made of. True love is not accidental. Love doesn't happen because Cupid hits you with his arrow. Love occurs because we let it. Love happens deliberately. Love occurs because we choose to love.

Often, teenagers like to justify their high school

romances with the excuse, "I just can't help it," or the even more sentimental line, "I can't live without him (or her)." Often adults believe this. Even adults may justify their own indiscretions with the same naïve excuse: "I just can't help it"; " I can't live without him."

People who believe that it is possible to "fall in love" and that we have no control over who we love, can get themselves into a world of trouble. Bishops who "fall in love" with Relief Society presidents, married men who "fall in love" with their secretaries, or teenagers who "fall in love" years before they are in a position to marry, all discover problems with the notion that love can't be controlled.

The misunderstanding that love just happens, unavoidably—while highly flattering when you're the object of all that love—isn't at all practical in real life. Man is given agency over his behavior and over his emotions. His agency isn't whisked away when it comes to love. Man must have control over his emotions, as well as his behavior, or our world would be in chaos.

The sentiment, "I've chosen to love you," might not make your heart leap when first whispered in your ear, however, such deliberate decision-making, when it comes to love, ought to provide a measure of comfort. The man who deliberately chooses to love is in control of his own feelings and is not at the mercy of a whim or a passing fantasy. How much more assured you can be that this calculated emotion will last. You don't need to worry that he will one day "fall in love" with someone other than you, claiming he couldn't control himself.

Teens who claim that they can't help themselves— that they fell in love without even knowing what was happening—recognize when they pause to think about their experience that they had every choice in the matter. They notice that "falling in love" is actually a process—a six-step process, I've discovered—that would more accurately be labeled, the "decision to love." These six steps are 1) longing, 2) looking, 3) focus, 4) flirting 5) exclusivity and 6) rose colored glasses. We have agency over every step in the process.

Six Steps to "Falling in Love"

1. LONGING

The choice to love begins with step one, a desire to be in a romantic relationship. Teenagers who "fall in love" actually begin longing for love well before they find it. Maybe you long for love because everyone else seems to have it. The love songs on the radio and the prevalence of romance movies in the theatre make you believe that there is only one purpose in life: to find love. Practically every song you hear (even on the non-country stations) drone on about looking for love, being in love, or losing a love. An alien tuning in to our media frequencies would think earthlings have nothing else to live for.

Maybe you long for a "one and only" because you're unhappy with your home life or because you feel insecure. Maybe it just looks alluring. Whatever the reason, longing for more than you have, longing for a boyfriend or girlfriend, is the first step in pursuing romantic love.

2. LOOKING

Looking for love is the next step. This is the step where you begin to compare what's available, with what you want. If looks are important to you, you will scan your school for the best-looking prospect. If intelligence is important, you'll look around for someone who is bright. If you merely want someone who is available, you're going to look around for somebody who isn't already in a relationship. Whatever it is that you want, you have to check out the prospects before you decide whom you want to focus on.

3. FOCUS

When you narrow your search down to individuals, you focus on them and only them. You pay attention to their schedule and make yourself available when they are available. You find out what they are interested in and develop an interest in the same things. You ask people what they know about the winner of your search. You daydream about him or her, and you forget all of the other prospects out there.

4. FLIRTING

The step after focus is flirting. This step might also be called "flirting with danger" if a teenager in no position to get serious reaches this step. Flirting is your attempt to get your crush to notice you. You might invite his notice through your physical presence, always hanging around his locker, his desk, or his car. You might invite her notice through cool clothes, long stares, or special attention to her comments or accomplishments. Flirting is an ancient art, and it is as easy to spot as black ink on a white shirt.

5. COUPLING

If the flirting produces results, your crush will return your affection and you will become a couple. This step of exclusivity needs to occur before love will truly flourish. Research has shown that human beings are created to be romantically involved with one person at a time. Therefore, before humans will allow themselves to fall in love, they want to be assured that they are the "only one." Or as the song says, "I only have eyes for you." Humans will hold back their affection if they think the object of their affection isn't going to be loyal to them. When they get a little bit of assurance that they are the only one, get out of the way.

6. WEARING ROSE-COLORED GLASSES

The last step to a love affair is focusing on the good and ignoring the bad. Young lovers have mastered this step. You may have heard the saying, "before marriage your beloved can do no wrong, and after marriage he can do no right." There is truth to this old adage. Couples in love are susceptible to the "pink lens effect," where they see everything through rose-colored glasses. It's easy to ignore faults at this point in a relationship, and love will flourish under these merciful conditions.

Falling in love feels like an accident, and it feels like it occurs in an instant, but in reality you have to open yourself up to the possibility. If you don't want to be in love, you can consciously refuse to participate in any of the steps that lead to love.

- You can decide you don't need a romantic relationship, and stop wishing you had one.

- Don't look around for a likely prospect for when you *are* old enough, or if you *were* in a position to have a boyfriend/girlfriend.

- Don't focus or flirt with just one person.

- And by all means, don't let one person know you like him/her.

You have the ability do of all of this. You have complete control over whether or not you fall in love. Teenagers who are years away from marriage should not even be looking for somebody to love.

Stopping at Any Step Along the Way

Our thoughts precede our deeds, always. We might not be aware of the thoughts that preceded our deeds, but if we can slow our thoughts down, we can pinpoint the moment when we started fantasizing, daydreaming, or wishing we had something we don't have. At this moment we can decide to control the longing.

Should you find yourself heading toward a love affair you have no business experiencing, put on the breaks the instant you recognize the path you are on. Even if you have slipped past the first step toward finding romance, then come to a dead stop before you reach the second step. If you catch yourself on the second step toward finding romance, you can come to a dead stop before you reach the third step. You can always stop flirting, stop hanging around your crush, or stop doing special things for him/her that you wouldn't normally do for anyone.

Teens can stop a romance by refusing to enter into an exclusive relationship. Going on casual dates with a lot of people is a guaranteed way to slow down a relationship and keep the love at a plutonic level.

Step six of a romance is a helpful step to be aware of because if you want to stop liking someone, it helps to look at your crush realistically, without the rose-colored glasses. An objective view of your crush, a view that acknowledges all the faults, character flaws, slights, and selfish behaviors, will put the brakes on an ill-timed love affair.

Choosing to Love

Forgive me if I have taken all the mystery out of romantic love—for popping a bubble that's filled with daydreams. Perhaps you'll now roll your eyes when you listen to love songs on the radio, or when you are cuddled up in front of a romantic movie, knowing that the couple you are watching is creating the romance, not mysteriously stumbling across it. As disappointing as it might be to discover that their romantic love does not occur magically, but deliberately, it should be equally reassuring that we can corral this wild emotion. A deliberate, informed attempt not to seek romantic love can protect you from ill-timed love affairs and reassure you that the real love affair in your future will last.

Chapter 10

It Will Not Last

AN IMPETUOUS LOVE AFFAIR, ONE WHERE YOU FALL without thinking, can end as quickly as it begins.

For those of you who are die-hard romantics who have bought into Hollywood's version of Romeo-and-Juliet-teen-love-at-first-sight (movies which are usually played by actors who are on their third our fourth marriages, by the way), let's play it this way. Check these facts: Out of 100 married people asked, 22 said they married their high school crush. Sounds great, huh? Maybe there is hope. But check this: Out of those 22 people, 17 got divorced. So 5 out of 100 people between the ages of 18 and 89 are still married to their high school sweethearts. Ouch! So you and your crush have two options—one, get married; two, break up.[1]

You can see from these statistics that there is a 95 percent chance of breaking up with your high school crush. If you had a million dollars and there was a 95 percent chance that you would lose it all if you invested it in the stock market, would you invest the million in the stock market? What if there was a more sure investment, someplace you could put your million dollars that there was a 95 percent chance that your money would grow incrementally forever? You'd be nuts to invest when the odds are 95 percent that you'll lose your money.

But that's exactly what you do if you fall in love in high school, go steady, and expect the relationship to last forever. You invest in a losing stock. On the other hand, there is sure way to make a huge return on your investment. Experience every step of the relationship funnel: don't skip friendship; don't skip casual dating. Take your time, and don't go steady until you are in a position to marry. Your investment will pay dividends you never imagined.

What about the 5 percent that stay married in the statistics quoted by DiMarco and Lookadoo? If any of you are big risk takers and willing to roll the dice and gamble that you'll be one of the 5 percent, you need to know something about that 5 percent. It includes couples who are eighty-nine years old! That means they married their high school sweetheart seventy years ago! Seventy years ago, couples who married young had a far better chance of staying together than they do today.

Back then it was easier to support a family without higher education. Nowadays it's really difficult. Back then all young men weren't instructed to go on missions like they are today. Half the Quorum of the Twelve didn't even serve missions (Monson, Eyring, Uchtdorf, Packer, Nelson, Oaks, and Hales). So the 5 percent who married young lived in a different world than we do today.

You can see from the following table that the median age for marriage has steadily increased over the past seventy years. Remember median means middle, so there were just as many people who were younger than the stated age as those who were older.

MEDIAN AGE AT FIRST MARRIAGE BY YEAR		
Year	Males	Females
1950	22.8	20.3
1960	22.8	20.3
1970	23.2	20.8
1980	24.7	22.0
1990	26.1	23.9
2000	26.8	25.1
2010	28.2	26.1

Source: US Census Bureau

Airplane Bias

When you see an elderly couple who met in high school and have been married for seventy years and are blissfully happy, you experience what I call "airplane bias." In one of my research methods classes in graduate school, we learned that many people are afraid to fly on airplanes because they fear the airplane will crash and everybody on board will be killed instantly. If you look at the actual statistics, few people die in airplane accidents compared to other types of accidents. However, the airplane accident is so dramatic, so traumatic that when it occurs it makes front-page news with double-sized headlines. People talk about it for days and years afterward. Because the news is "big news" we think it's "broad news." Big and broad are not the same thing. The news is significant in size, but it is not significant in scope. It doesn't happen often and it doesn't happen to many people, but when it does happen, it's a truly noteworthy event.

Airplane bias occurs when we look at successful high school romances. We may get the impression that high school romances make it all the time just because we know one really unique couple that made it.

One of the most famous examples of the 5 percent is that of Elder Groberg who was supposedly saved from drowning by the love of a girl from home. Apparently Hollywood added a little drama to *The Other Side of Heaven* that leads youth to an erroneous conclusion.

Elder Groberg himself said,

> While I was serving in Tonga, Jean [now his wife] fulfilled callings in the Church, continued her schooling, graduated and began teaching school. She dated other fine young men during those years and was proposed to by someone else, but chose to wait until I returned. I think the Lord expects us to get acquainted with many others so we know how we react to various personalities, attitudes, testimonies, etc.
>
> I feel there is no conflict with the experience Jean and I had and the teachings of the prophets, and I hope you help bring the young people you work with to see no conflict either.[2]

Elder Groberg isn't even among the 5 percent. Jean was still dating other guys while he was on his mission. High school romances that last seventy years are like airplane crashes. They don't occur very often, but when they do, they make front-page news, with double-sized headlines.

Most high school relationships are more like fender-benders than airplane crashes. They happen to practically everybody who's ever had a driver's license. Few of them last. And it's not front-page news. Fender benders don't make headlines even though they personally affect far more people than an airplane crash ever will.

Breaking Up Because of Moral Issues

Since people marry later these days, the odds against successful marriage to a high school sweetheart continue to mount. Too many obstacles face young lovers who dream of staying together for a lifetime. One of the toughest challenges teenagers face, if they have high standards of morality, is the temptation to have sex.

We already know that teens who are dating seriously are three times more likely to have sex than those dating casually.[3]

A study conducted by anthropologist Helen Fisher found that 73 percent of men and 65 percent of women daydreamed about having sex with their beloved. She also studied poetry that attested to the lover's "intense craving for sexual union with the beloved."[4]

Imagine a guy and a girl fall in love when they are sixteen years of age, and one or both of them believes in waiting until marriage to have sex. The longer they are in a romantic relationship, the hotter their passions flame. By the time they are seventeen or eighteen years old, they are comfortable with one another, and they are sexually attracted to one another. But they certainly can't marry at seventeen or eighteen. In reality, marriage isn't feasible until they are twenty-two or twenty-three years old. That means they have to be in a loving, longing-for-sex relationship for *five* years and not consummate that love. It will take an act of God to keep them from having sex before marriage.

No matter how strong a couple's moral values, no matter how determined to "save themselves" until marriage, few couples can withstand that kind of temptation. They can't spend all kinds of time with one another, gazing into one another's eyes, whispering sweet nothings into one another's ear, and then shake hands on the doorstep. They are going to desire, crave, and long for a sexual union. This leaves them with one of two choices: they either violate their moral standards and go ahead and have sex, or they break up because it's the only way they have a prayer of withstanding the temptation to have sex. Do you see how teen romance is doomed to failure?

Going Separate Ways

As much as you think you will be able to keep your relationship strong across the miles or across the years, it just doesn't seem to happen. The quintessential example of breaking up because of going separate ways is the "Dear John" letter. This occurrence is so common that we actually have a name for the rejection letter.

Although President Benson said clear back in 1986 to "avoid steady dating with a young man prior to the time of his mission call,"[5] some youth still confuse *Saturday's Warrior* for gospel truth and think it's okay to wait for a missionary.

The truth is, no young man can be a good missionary and a good boyfriend at the same time. If he is a good missionary, concentrating on the work, he will neglect his girlfriend and cause her undue worry. If he is a good boyfriend, paying attention to the girlfriend and their relationship, he won't be able to function as a missionary.

Too many young people have to learn this fact the hard

way. A young lady discovers that "out of sight" indeed does mean "out of mind" and she is enticed by all the young men who are available to date while the boy she supposedly loves is gone. She soon writes him a "Dear John" letter, suggesting they end their relationship. Young men who desire to be excellent missionaries quickly realize that a girlfriend at home is a distraction and they can't focus on the work with that kind of a distraction. So he writes her a "Dear Jane."

Going away to college can cause a rift in the relationship as well. Both guys and girls are excited about all the new people they are meeting and all the new friends they are making. Pretty soon, one of those friends becomes more than a friend, and the girlfriend or boyfriend back home is forgotten.

Breaking Up Because of Selfishness

Just because adolescents claim they are in love does not mean they know how to love well. Scott Peck (author of *The Road Less Traveled*) said true love is about caring for the spiritual welfare of another being. Few adolescents have the capacity to love in a caring, selfless, non-exploitive manner. True love wants the best for the other person. True lovers will sacrifice their own pleasure to meet the essential needs of the other person.

Teens are developmentally unprepared to succeed in an intimate, long-term relationship. They are just too selfish. And that's okay. Selfishness in adolescence is developmentally normal.

"*The self-focused level is the first level of relationship maturity, at which one's perspective of another or a relationship is concerned only with how it affects the self.* The individual's own wishes and plans overshadow those of others, and the individual shows little concern for others"[6]

Selfishness and committed relationships don't go well together at all. There is no way a committed relationship will last when one or both partners are inherently selfish.

> Marriage . . . means sacrifice, sharing, and even a reduction of some personal liberties. It means long, hard economizing. It means children who bring with them financial burdens, service burdens, carry and worry burdens . . . before marriage, each individual is quite free to go and come as he pleases, to organize and plan his life as it seems best, to make all decisions with self as the central point.[7]

I grew up with five brothers. They were all big boys— literally twice my size. When dinnertime came you had to race to the table because if you were a minute late, there wouldn't be anything left to eat.

When I got married, I half expected my husband to act the same way. I remember the first time I discovered how different marriage was. I had made a derby pie, and there was only one slice left. We finished our dinner one night and I suggested we flip a coin to see who got the last piece of pie. He refused. "No. You have it," he offered. "You love chocolate. I want you to have it." I was shocked. I was completely unused to having a man put me before himself.

He continued to behave in this chivalrous manner. If we left the movies and it was pouring rain outside, he would run and get the car, bring it up to the curb, and open the door so I could stay dry. Often we would fall into bed late at night, both exhausted and desperate for sleep.

Suddenly I would spout, "Oh, no. I left the lights on in the garage." My husband would jump up and go turn them off. When the toilet got clogged, he's the one who pulled out the plunger and cleaned it out. Our marriage became a contest not over who could get the most from the other but who could *do* the most for one another.

This is the opposite of the behavior seen in teenage relationships:

"I can't afford the gas. You need to drive."

"We went to your dumb movie last week. I want to see mine this week."

"You always go off with your friends and never spend time with me."

"You can afford new hubcaps, but you can't afford to take me to dinner."

Few adolescents have matured to the point that they are more concerned for the other person than they are for themselves. Most adolescents love because it feels good to them.

Nobody, at any age, has any business being in a relationship if they can't sacrifice. Therefore, teenage relationships are doomed to failure because teenagers aren't mature enough to make the sacrifices necessary to succeed in a romantic, intimate relationship. It's like putting an adolescent in the pilot's seat of a commercial airplane and asking them to fly to London. They don't know how to fly and the consequences of their lack of knowledge could be disastrous.

Breaking Up Because of Boredom

Teenage relationships are also likely to break up because the novelty wears off. Romantic relationships ignite because dopamine in the brain increases and adrenaline soars, and lovers feel a physiological high just thinking about one another.[8] This high, however, wears off. It can't last. Humans would not be able to function if the ecstasy they feel when they first fall in love remained in a long-term relationship. Lovers in the passionate stage can't concentrate on anything except one another, and so they spend inordinate amounts of time together. If this "lovers high" lasted for fifty years, no one would live a productive life by building a career or contributing to mankind.

True love can last a lifetime, but it's not the same feeling teenagers urgently embrace during the early months of their love affair. Young people, who don't understand the life-cycle of romance, think that when the passion wears off that their love isn't real. They then choose to end the romantic relationship in search of a new, fresh, exciting relationship. Teenagers are too inexperienced to know that all romantic passion changes its form and turns into another kind of love. Therefore, teens will give up on their boyfriend or girlfriend in search of a relationship that will allow them to re-create the emotional high found in the early stages of romance. So teenage love affairs die, not because the love wasn't real, but because the youth don't know what real love looks like and think they need to continue their quest.

I believe one of the messages conveyed in Shakespeare's famous play *Romeo and Juliet* is that adolescent romance is doomed to failure. Romeo and Juliet are star-crossed lovers, not simply because their parents are feuding, but because it isn't in the stars for thirteen-year-olds to be together. The impetuosity of youth ultimately kills them both. (You probably studied this play in ninth grade, the very age at which teenagers are trying on adult relationships. But I'll bet your teacher didn't teach you that Romeo and Juliet were too young to be that serious in the first place.)

Die-hard romantics want to believe that love conquers all—opposition, obstacles, and even death. We, who have been nourished with a diet of *Sleeping Beauty*, *Snow White*, and *Beauty and the Beast*, might believe that lovers can overcome any adversity—poison spindles, poison apples, and hexes and curses of all varieties. Intrinsic within every romantic fairy tale is a couple in love who stay together against all odds.

This is what DiMarco and Lookadoo have to say to those die-hard romantics.

I know. I know. I'm wrong about *your* relationship. It's different. You are the exception. You're right for each other. You can just feel it. You have so much in common. You like the same movies. You know each other so deeply that you even finish each other's sentences. You know what the other is thinking. It hurts when you're apart. Congrats! But that has nothing to do with it. . . . Just because you *believe* your relationship is different doesn't mean it is. . . . I may believe I don't have to wear clothes to school, but that doesn't mean I'm right.[9]

Young lovers who insist their relationship is going to last forever are the only ones who are surprised when it doesn't.

Have Faith

If you really believe you've found your soul mate in high school, test your hypothesis. Stay friends until after your mission and if you are really meant to be together, then you can begin your romance. If you did make a deal in the pre-existence (I have NO idea if that even happens) and agreed to spend mortality together, then it will happen. You don't need to "reserve" your beloved while you are teenagers. He or she will still be there when you become adults.

I dated a boy in high school who was the dearest of friends. He dated lots of girls and he even kept track of how many girls he dated, giving us each a number. This guy really believed in doing his homework, so he dated lots of girls casually. I was number 25. We had fun together, and I had a great deal of respect for him. After high school, he went on his mission, and when he came home, we started dating again. This time he wasn't just casually dating, he was looking for a wife. By now I was number fifty. Seriously. He was going to look the world over for the right woman. He eventually found her. It wasn't me. I'm not sure what number she was. But they were totally compatible and have a very happy marriage.

I have always thought the following saying provided excellent advice, "If you love something very, very much, let it go free. If it does not return, it was never meant to be yours. If it does, love it forever."

Endnotes

1. Justin Lookadoo and Hayley DiMarco, *Datable: are you? Are they?* Grand Rapids, MI: Baker House Co., 2003, 13.

2. John H. Groberg, letter to the author, Nov. 3 2005.

3. Associated Press, "Holidays tempt teens to have sex, study says," *The Florida Times Union*, Dec. 25, 2002, A-9.

4. Helen Fisher, *Why We Love: The Nature and Chemistry of Romantic Love*. New York: Henry Holt and Company, 2004, 20.

5. Ezra T. Benson, "To the Young Women of the Church," *Ensign*, Nov. 1986, 82-83.

6. John Santrock, *Life-Span Development*. Dubuque, IA: William C. Brown Publishers, 2004, 507. Emphasis added.

7. Spencer W. Kimball, "Marriage and Divorce," *BYU Speeches*, Sept. 7, 1976, 142-55.

8. Pat Love, *The Truth about Love*, New York: Simon & Schuster Inc., 2001, 29.

9. Justin Lookadoo and Hayley DiMarco, *Datable: are you? Are they?* Grand Rapids, MI: Baker House Co., 2003, 13.

Chapter 11

Achy Breaky Heart

Because high school romances do not last, those who insist on trying them are doomed to break up. We use the term "break" for a reason when describing a breakup. Something really does break, shattering like a window smashed by a baseball or a crystal vase hurled onto a tile floor. But that thing that breaks is far more valuable than a crystal vase or a window. The thing that breaks is your heart.

I have some friends who asked me to share the story of their fourteen-year-old daughter, Diane. Diane developed a relationship with a young man on the Internet who was fifteen, a year older than she was. They sent texts to one another constantly and spent hours on the telephone and on the computer, pouring out their hearts to one another. At fourteen, Diane was deeply in love. Then her boyfriend turned sixteen. Suddenly he was old enough to go on dates. So even though they had never even gone on a date, he broke up with Diane and found a new girlfriend—a girlfriend he could actually take someplace.

Diane was devastated. She slipped into a deep depression. For weeks she wouldn't come out of her room, and she refused to eat. She rapidly dropped weight to the point where her parents were alarmed enough to take her to the doctor. The doctor, equally alarmed, discovered that Diane had anorexia nervosa and required hospitalization.

Diane's first mistake was to develop an exclusive relationship before she was old enough to be in an exclusive relationship. But her mental illness began when the person to whom she had entrusted her heart carelessly and casually discarded it.

Gordon B. Hinckley told a story about when he was a little boy. He said, "we traded paper hearts at school, and at night we dropped them at the doors of our friends, stamping on the porch and then running in the dark to hide. Sometimes we would tie a fishing line to a valentine, and when the would-be receiver would go to pick it up we would pull the string. That happens in life with some of us."[1]

Distractions

The response to a breakup will range from mild to severe. Even breakups less traumatic than Diane's can set you back and slow you down on your way to accomplishing your goals.

My youngest son recently returned from a mission to Ecuador. One of the elders in his mission broke the mission rules and logged on to Facebook. On Facebook he saw pictures of his girlfriend with another boy. He was so upset that he actually left the mission and went back home so he could monitor her.

One of my friends taught high school English for years, and one of her course requirements was that the students keep a journal. In reading these journals she learned about every love affair in the high school. She knew who was getting dumped, and by whom. She says, "The correlation between their academic performance and the state of their love affairs was astounding."

When I was a student, one of the smartest guys in our school suddenly stopped coming to class. For weeks he was absent, and nobody knew where he was. We didn't know if he had been in an accident, or if he had moved. We were all quite concerned. Finally, after more than a month he returned to school. It turned out that his girlfriend had dumped him, and he was so upset, he couldn't even face those people who still liked him.

The more serious the relationship, the more effecting the breakup. A couple who has been together for a long time and had high hopes for their relationship will fall harder than a couple who dated seriously for only a short period of time, without the expectation that the relationship would last.

Anger

One of the ways adolescents respond to a breakup is with anger. The anger adolescents experience at "being dumped" can be pretty scary. Psychologists call this stage of grief after a breakup "abandonment rage."[2]

One of my clients had to have her car repainted two times because her ex-boyfriend kept keying the paint job. She called the police because she knew full well who had done it, but because he was not caught in the act, she was stuck with the expensive repair bills. Another angry adolescent slashed the tires of her boyfriend's car. Not only was this expensive, but it was potentially very dangerous. Fistfights among boys and catfights among girls are not uncommon when adolescents feel their true love has been "stolen away" by another.

A study conducted by researchers at Cornell University and the University of Georgia discovered that stalking is a common problem when relationships end. Over 600 undergraduates participated in the study, and over 20 percent reported that their exes continued to bother them with phone calls, watching their residence, following them, or threatening physical harm.[3]

Erika Harold, 2002 Miss America, won on a platform of youth violence prevention. She advocated staying away from illegal drugs and alcohol because they are big risk factors for teen violence. However, another lesser known risk factor is teen sex. Miss Harold stressed sexual abstinence because statistics show that teens who are sexually active are more likely to be victims of violence than those who are not.[4]

Violence occurs in one out of three teenage relationships. "National surveys have estimated that one in three youths experiences dating abuse at some time during their teens."[5]

It's one thing to have your lover "be crazy about you" but quite another to have him go crazy because of you.

Shame

Tragically, adolescents often feel because they were "dumped" that there is something wrong with them. Shame may be one of the most common emotions I see when youth come in for therapy. These precious youth believe they are inadequate, unlovable, or deficient, all because of the immaturity of a single teenager.

When you've been dumped, it can affect your self-esteem to the point that you won't reach out and pursue other friendships. You may turn down opportunities to try out for clubs, compete in contests, or run for office because you feel terrible about yourself. Adolescence is a time when human beings have a pretty hard time feeling adequate anyway, and then when someone, whom you thought had a clue, tells you, "you are not good enough for me," it can whack your sense of worth right off its foundation.

The older we are, the better our ability to deal with rejection. If a relationship ends when we are more sure of ourselves, we can usually keep our self-esteem intact.

Adolescence, however, is the absolute worst time of life to deal with a breakup because the human identity is still forming. Adolescents aren't always sure about who they are or don't always feel good about who they think they are; they are just developing an identity, and that work is not finished.

"Forming an identity, like building a theory, is a creative endeavor that takes much time and concentrated effort. That is why Erikson has suggested that teenagers either make or find a 'moratorium,' a period of time for themselves during which they can engage in the task of identity formation."[6] Incidentally, an LDS mission is an excellent moratorium.

The irony is that the teenagers who are desperate for a relationship often want one to increase their self-esteem . . . and look what happens! The relationship ends up messing with their self-esteem more than if they never had a boyfriend or girlfriend.

Depression

Symptoms of depression can range from shedding a few tears to a major depressive episode. The more mild consequences of an adolescent breakup might be sadness. Significant levels of sadness can turn into depression.

One man describes his depression this way, "I crashed and burned for nearly three months before I realized that I was going to live and that this moping around was no excuse for living. I decided that it would be wonderful if I found someone who would share my life, but I wasn't going to live or die depending on her decision to love me."[7]

Depression in an adolescent may look different than it does in adults. While you often see radical changes in eating and sleeping habits, like you do with adult depression, adolescents may experience more anger or acting out. Your parents might think you're just a bad kid, when really you're experiencing depression.

Depressed adolescents can be impulsive, reacting on the spur of the moment, without giving themselves time to reason. The Columbine tragedy that took place in 1999 in Colorado is an example of the disaster that can occur when we see a combination of emotional immaturity, trauma, and impulsive behavior.

Research on adolescent suicidal behavior has also revealed that one of the reasons adolescents attempt to take their own lives is that they were in a serious relationship that ended in a breakup.[8] They may want to hurt the person that dropped them, and they believe their suicide will make the offending partner hurt as much as they hurt.

In the spring of 2004, one of my son's classmates jumped off a building in downtown Jacksonville. She was an honor student, had an academic scholarship to a university, was a popular student, and was involved in a number of activities. But when her boyfriend broke up with her, she committed suicide. The article in the paper quoted the principal who said, "Kids are under a lot of stress in this day and age. Relationships are a big issue with kids."[9]

If you've ever been so sad that you contemplated suicide, see a doctor! Please. If you can't get an appointment right away, go to the emergency room. Even if you don't really plan to act on those suicidal thoughts, the fact that you are having them is a sign that you are seriously sad. You shouldn't have to stick it out alone. There are wonderful professionals who know how and want to help, and it makes a world of difference.

I Can Handle It

Adolescence is full of risk takers who like speed, height, and adrenaline surges. Therefore, they often choose to engage in potentially dangerous behavior. They take these chances because they believe that bad things

1. will *never* happen to me, or
2. I *can* handle it.

I applied this very same logic recently when my husband had a nasty head cold. Usually I take great care not to get sick, so when he has a cold, I refuse to kiss him until he's better. This time I took a chance. I thought

1. it won't happen to me, and
2. if it does, I can handle it.

Several days after I applied this "illogical logic," I came down with a terrible sore throat. It felt like needles were jabbing into me. My head ached like I had hit it on a boulder and my body shivered with fever. "What an idiot," I thought to myself. And I realized two very important things

1. it *will* happen to me, and
2. I don't *want* to handle it.

I hope it doesn't take something akin to fever and chills to convince you that you don't particularly like getting dumped.

Pain Avoidance

Granted, breakups may be part of life, but they are less likely if couples are (1) mature enough to treat one another appropriately, and (2) in a position to get married.

Couples who are old enough to date seriously, and are in a position to marry, may still find that after steadily dating, they are not meant for one another. They need to end the relationship, but they do not need to break one another's hearts.

A breakup is usually one person's idea, and although it may cause both of them distress, it is most painful to the person who didn't want the relationship to end. This is the person who is shattered, crushed, and devastated. The one getting dumped is usually the one who will experience the pain we associate with breakups.

The solution is for neither person to get dumped. Both members of the couple need to agree, together, at the same time to end the relationship. If one of you realizes the relationship isn't going to last, gently help the other person recognize what you already see. First talk about the relationship, highlighting your incompatibilities, your different goals, the reasons it isn't likely to last. Ideally, you will both see the same things about the relationship. Then together you can decide the best way to handle this information. Hopefully, you will both realize it's smartest to end the relationship, and neither of you feels cast away.

This is a tip you may not need until you are in college and dating somebody seriously. But just in case you entered a serious relationship too early, you can use the tip right now and avoid heartache.

Endnotes

1. Gordon B. Hinckley, "And the greatest of These Is Love," *BYU Speeches*, Feb. 14, 1978.

2. Helen Fisher, "Broken Hearts: The Nature Risks of Romantic Rejection," *Romance and Sex in Adolescence and Emerging Adulthood, Risks and Opportunities* edited by Ann Crouter and Alan Booth, New York: Routledge, 2006, 14.

3. J. Haugaard, *Criminal Justice and Behavior*, Feb. 2004: vol. 31, 37-54.

4. Betsy Hart, "What? Miss America can't preach abstinence," *Deseret News*, Oct. 13, 2002, AA4.

5. David Crary, "Report: States lag in dating-violence laws," *Florida Times Union*, Mar. 24, 2009, A-5.

6. David Elkind, *All Grown Up and No Place to Go*, Boston: Da Capo Press, 1998, 9.

7. Gawain and Gale Wells, "Courtship: Labor of Love," *Ensign*, Dec. 1979, 22.

8. American Academy of Pediatrics, accessed on Feb. 13, 2012, aappolicy.aappublications.org/cgi/content/full/pediatrics;105/4/

9. Drew Dixon, "Deaths of students send grief through Nease High halls," *Ponte Vedra Shorelines,* Mar. 27, 2004, 1.

Chapter 12

Gender Differences

I READ RECENTLY ABOUT SOME PARENTS FROM TORONTO who were trying a social experiment on their child. They wanted to hide all trace of gender. They gave their child an androgynous name like Storm. They dressed their child in generic colors—green or yellow instead of the traditional pink or blue. They cut the child's hair in a way that wouldn't reveal if the child was a boy or a girl. Their hope is that the child will develop a gender identity without being influenced by the world.[1]

The entire idea made me laugh out loud. Any parent who thinks that gender tendencies are created by our environment rather than our genetics has never had children. Boys and girls are so different you don't even have to change their diapers to be able to discern the difference.

Marriage therapists have saved hundreds and thousands of marriages over the years by revealing this fact: men are from Mars, and women are from Venus. Men are told, "if you just accept that your wife is not like you and that does not mean she is defective, you'll be far more content." Women are told, "Stop trying to change your husband to make him more like you. He wasn't made that way." One of my most popular talks at BYU Education Week is about gender differences. We instinctively recognize gender differences, and it's nice to have them validated.

Throughout this book, I have written as if guys and girls face the same challenges when it comes to avoiding exclusive relationships in high school. While every one of the principles taught heretofore does apply to both genders, it is as obvious as the morning following the night that boys and girls face different challenges in avoiding exclusive relationships.

You've learned that both emotional and physical intimacy propel a relationship from the friendship stage into the romance stage. What I haven't stated, but what you may suspect, is that one gender usually pushes for emotional intimacy, and the other for physical intimacy. Can you guess which is which? Of course you can.

Consider the following poem revealing vast differences in a relationship.

You forgive me for liking you too much,
And I'll forgive you for not liking me enough.

You forgive me for missing you so,
And I'll forgive you for being so cold.

You forgive me for the loud racing of my heart,
And I'll forgive you for not hearing it.

You forgive me for playing your games,

And I'll forgive you for toying with my emotions.

You forgive me for finding you so attractive,
And I'll forgive you for not noticing.

You forgive me for raising you up so high,
And I'll forgive you for bringing me down so low.

You forgive me for wanting to be with you,
And I'll forgive you for avoiding me.

You forgive me for being so pathetic,
And I'll forgive you for taking advantage of it.

You forgive me for not being able to let go,
And I'll forgive you for never having latched on.

You forgive me for having hopes and dreams,
And I'll forgive you for crushing them.

Forgiveness brings inner peace.
Do we have a deal?

Who wrote this poem? Was it a boy or a girl? Before I even tell you the author's name is Melissa, there is no doubt whatsoever that the poem was written by a girl.

Granted, we are working off a stereotype here. There may be sensitive guys out there who want a relationship, and girls who prefer independence. But statistically speaking, it's the girls who push for emotional intimacy in a relationship, while the boys push for physical intimacy.

This is cool. There's nothing wrong with you if you're a girl who wants emotional intimacy, and there's nothing wrong with you if you're a guy who wants physical intimacy. This is normal. It's how men and women come together. You just have to wait. Intimacy must wait, whichever type you long for.

Bargaining

At the beginning of a relationship, couples use these gender differences to "bargain" with one another in order to have their own personal needs met.

The girls don't come right out and say, "If I give you sex, do you agree to love me?" Neither do the boys say, "If I love you, will you give me sex?" Whether or not they speak it aloud, the relationship follows this unspoken rule.

Girls feel that if she gives a boy a kiss, he is required to be exclusive with her. If he flirts with another girl, or—heaven-forbid—kisses another girl, the first girl feels betrayed. The girl expects an emotional commitment from the boy she kissed. She expects their relationship to be at a more serious level emotionally because the relationship became more serious physically.

Boys, on the other hand, may not recognize this expectation, or they may not wish to comply with this expectation. Boys generally want a kiss because it feels good physically. They don't need a serious relationship, they don't want a serious relationship, or they may be totally afraid of a serious relationship. They just want a kiss. However, in order to get that kiss, the boy discovers he needs to comply with the girl's expectations. He may be reluctant, or he may even be insincere, but the boy gives in and allows himself to become more emotionally involved than he initially desires, because that's the way he gets his physical needs met.

The old Beach Boys song echoes this age-old truth: "All the guys go steady because it wouldn't be right to leave your best girl home on a Saturday night." Going steady isn't the guys' first choice, but they agree to abide by the rules of the relationship: She gives physical affection to him, he remains faithful to her.

Use This Knowledge

Now that you know how the relationship dance works, you can make more deliberate choices about how your relationship progresses. Girls, because physical intimacy isn't all that important to you right now, you have power to control how far the relationship goes physically. This doesn't mean that boys aren't responsible for how far the relationship goes physically. It means that girls have more power. They are not as influenced by this drive for physical intimacy, so it is easier for them to put on the breaks. The boys feel powerless (although they aren't) when it comes to resisting physical intimacy. Because this is so much more difficult for the boys, and so much easier for the girls, the girls have more say over how far the relationship goes physically.

On the other hand, teenage boys generally aren't driven by the desire for emotional intimacy. Many claim they don't ever want to grow up and would be delighted if Neverland really existed. Therefore, it is easier for the boys to keep a casual relationship from becoming too emotionally intimate. This does not mean girls do not have the responsibility to curb their desire for emotional intimacy; it means because its easier for the boys, they should step up to the plate and do their part. Guys, you need to be honest here. Because emotional intimacy isn't really a driving force at this time in your life, do not pretend that you are totally into being emotionally intimate just to get the girl.

Rules Change

Although at the beginning of a relationship boys and girls are driven by different needs that help them come together, the rules change once the relationship becomes a solid romance that could lead to marriage. No longer do boys consider emotional intimacy an unnecessary nuisance. Once they give their hearts away, boys can love as deeply as any woman. Likewise, after marriage, women can have as great a desire for physical intimacy as their husbands do.

Bargaining does not need to take place in a healthy marital relationship because in a marriage a couple has reached the point where they freely give themselves to one another, both emotionally and physically. However, when a relationship is first beginning, male-female needs differ, and knowing the difference will help you control how serious the relationship gets.

A searing story reveals gender differences in their ugliest form. A straight-A student who attended my son's high school became pregnant by a senior on the school's football team. The football player actually gave the girl's name, address, and phone number to the entire team. He said, "If you are out of her house by five thirty, you can visit her any afternoon before her parents get home because she doesn't know how to say no."[2]

A girl who can't say no wants to be loved. She doesn't want to hurt anybody's feelings. She wants to make everybody happy. That's her nature. A boy who simply wants sex doesn't care a whit about the person with whom he has sex. He is striving strictly to meet a physical need.

These two different needs lie at opposite ends of a spectrum. Selfish sex is at one extreme, and love given to one's personal detriment is at the other extreme.

Gender Bargaining

Sex ——————Mutual Fulfillment ————Love
(Boys want)   (Girls want)

While the boy who desires only sex is still learning how to love, and the girl who desires only love is learning that there is such thing as non-exploitive sex, the couple are worlds apart in their ability to negotiate a healthy, intimate, fulfilling relationship.

Eventually, mature adults learn to meet someplace in the middle. However, while living in these separate worlds, boys and girls have absolutely no business meeting. Both the boy and the girl have an enormous capacity to hurt one another.

A Word about Boys

Girls need to understand that a teenage boy, by nature, is far more interested in sex than he is in love. This may be difficult to comprehend because a girl doesn't think the same way as a boy. It is difficult to understand someone who is so different than you are.

My male clients have helped me understand what it's like to be a young boy filled with testosterone. "You don't think about sex on occasion," they insist, their fists balled, and their eyes rolling in a circle. "You think about sex 100 percent of the time. You can't shake it. It's practically impossible to concentrate."

If these boys are telling me the truth, and out of respect

for them I have to believe they are, then keeping their thoughts pure must pose a tremendous challenge. One can only imagine what it's like for them to look at girls who dress provocatively and not to think impure thoughts. It must be even more difficult to be in a relationship with a girl who is pushing for emotional intimacy, hugging, and kissing, and expecting him not to think about sex.

Teenage boys don't want a relationship like the girls want. They want to race mountain bikes, fly off ski jumps, and travel around the world. They want adventure, sex too, but not commitment. They don't want to settle down. They want to soar.

Girls, you need to know how guys tend to think. The girl who thinks a guy is interested in her, when he is only interested in one thing, can make a total fool of herself by throwing her heart at someone who will not catch it. Have the dignity to save your heart for a young man who has grown up, who is mature, who is ready to settle down, and who wants a commitment.

Girls may disparage guys with comments like, "All guys are dogs," when guys are just being guys. Although boys should never exploit a girl for sex, girls who expect commitment of high school boys are setting themselves up for disappointment. Teenage girls who want a teenage boy to settle down and be faithful are asking him to do something that is against his nature.

All about Girls

Guys need to understand gender differences as well. The temptation girls face during adolescent years is not to become too physically intimate, but to become too emotionally intimate.

Guys need to accept the fact that girls don't crave sex the way they do. A girl who shows interest in them doesn't want to be used; she wants to be loved. She wants commitment and caring and permanency. She will not be happy with a one-night stand. She will feel used and angry.

Some young men justify their sexual pursuit of a girl with excuses like, "She wanted it too," or "I didn't hear her complaining." While in reality, she is bargaining, trying to get a commitment from him.

Boys must be honest with themselves regarding their willingness to commit. Many a "player" has convinced a girl that he will be exclusive with her, and that he truly desires commitment, only to get the physical affection he craves. As soon as he gets his physical needs satisfied, he goes back on his agreement to be exclusive and plays the same game with another girl (perhaps this is where he earned the label "player").

Some girls, in an effort to not feel "used," might try to convince themselves that they are as sexual as the guys, and that the relationship really is fair when they give a guy what he wants sexually. While there may be some statistical outliers who truly crave sex, girls who rationalize that sex is as good for them as it is for the boys are fooling themselves. There is nothing equal about a boy's and a girl's sex drive. Once girls recognize this truth, their rationalizations vanish and their reason begins to reign.

Some high school boys may delude themselves into thinking they are ready for a real relationship, with commitment and caring and fidelity. They may actually pursue a girl, thinking they can be faithful, and they can be faithful forever. Once again, they soon discover that relationships require a lot more than they imagined, and they bail out on the girl and on their promises.

Boys who are honest in their relationships and truly keep their commitments are called gentlemen. They have "honorable intentions" and they only ask young ladies to give as great a physical commitment as they are willing and able to give emotionally.

In Tolstoy's classic novel *Anna Karenina* we meet a villain who gleefully disregards social norms. We learn that in Russia in 1910, a young man was expected to have honorable intentions when he called on a young lady. Nevertheless, Vronsky, who later seduces Anna Karenina, first seduces a young girl named Kitty.

Tolstoy writes: "He did not know that this mode of behavior in relation to Kitty had a definite character, that it is courting young girls with no intentions of marriage, and that such courting is one of the evil actions common among brilliant young men such as he was. It seemed to him that he was the first who had discovered this pleasure, and he was enjoying his discovery." [3]

In Tolstoy's novel, the motive for his seduction was not necessarily to meet physical needs. In this case, he was intoxicated by his power and arrogant about his own attractiveness.

Literature reveals universal emotions, universal experiences. Books teach us lessons that can spare us from real-life pain. Hopefully these classics will help you understand that these gender differences occur across cultures and across time.

In William Thackary's *Vanity Fair*, we witness George Osborne toying with Amelia Sedley, to whom he is engaged, but unwilling to commit. Sitting by the drawing room window with a "sad, wistful face," Amelia is being stood up by her fiancé, yet again. Amelia "waited and waited but George never came." In describing Amelia's shame, Thackary says, "Poor little tender heart! And so it goes on hoping and beating, and longing and trusting. You see it is not much of a life to describe. There is not much of what you call incident in it. Only one feeling all day—when will he come? Only one thought to sleep and wake upon." [4]

Stories of women trusting and men taking advantage of that trust abound in literature.

Willa Cather tells of a brave heroine in the book *My Antonia*. A Bohemian immigrated to Nebraska from Czechoslovakia, Antonia flourished on pioneer land. Antonia's flaw was she trusted a rake. "She won't hear a word against him. She's so sort of innocent," the neighbors said. "If she once likes people, she won't hear anything against them." [5]

Responding to an invitation for marriage to the very man she had been warned about, Antonia leaves for Denver. Months later, she returns unmarried, pregnant, and alone, and entirely unwilling to go out in public. Late one night, she went into her room behind the kitchen and shut the door. "There, without calling to anybody, without a groan, she lay down on the bed and bore her child."

How sad to be like Antonia, refusing to heed the objective perspective of those all around you, only to find out later that the perspective was accurate all along.

The lessons we learn from reading are vital. Heed them. Don't be in too big a hurry to be in an exclusive relationship. Wait until the time is right. Then you can experience love that really will last for eternity.

Endnotes

1. Tom Blackwell, "Toronto parents hide child's gender

in bid for neutral treatment," *National Post*, May 25, 2011.

2. *Ponte Vedra Shorelines*, Oct. 7, 2006, 1.

3. Leo Tolstoy, *Anna Karenina*, New York: Random House, 2000, 67-68.

4. William Thackary, *Vanity Fair*, New York: Alfred A. Knopf, 1991, 110.

5. Willa Cather, *My Antonia*, Houghton Mifflin, 1949, 268.

Chapter 13

Role Models

I wish I could suggest some good role models for you to follow. It would be helpful to observe teens who have learned how to date unsteadily and are enjoying wonderful friendships. I have scoured contemporary movies and books and listened to the songs on the radio, without much success. Every time I see a great movie in which a teenage boy and a girl are developing a wonderful friendship, it turns into a romance before the movie ends.

Too many people seem to believe the famous quote by playwright Oscar Wilde, "Between men and women there is no friendship." Wilde claims that men and women who are in a friendship will always become sexually attracted to one another, and will not have the will power to resist that attraction.[1]

This is a rather insulting view of human nature. It makes human beings sound like animals, with absolutely no self-control, driven by instincts and drives and unable to tame those drives. Of course, men and women can be friends without becoming romantic. You just have to make that choice.

Proving Yourself

Unlike animals, you can exercise your agency. You prove it all the time. For example, what if one of your same-gender friends has a boyfriend or girlfriend? Do you hook up with your friend's boyfriend or girlfriend because you simply can't help it? If so you're certain to lose your friend. You refrain from romantic notions because you know romance is "out of the question." You're simply not going there. It's not going to happen. You might even be better friends with your friend's boyfriend or girlfriend than they are because you both have dismissed the very possibility of a romance.

Tell yourself, "There is no chance of this becoming a romance. Don't even think of it," and you can be reassured that friendships will remain friendships.

You have proven that you can refrain from rushing into romance in other situations as well. If you have a job where fraternization is prohibited (you're not allowed to date each other) or you will lose your job, you decide from the beginning that your relationships will remain friendships. If romance even crosses your mind, you simply dismiss the thought by saying to yourself, "don't even think of it." Recall the example I gave from when I served on the seminary council. We weren't allowed to seriously date one another or we would get kicked off the council. So we didn't even think of it.

Missionaries are off-limits to dating. Therefore, (if you have an ounce of integrity) you won't even consider trying to date a missionary. You won't flirt, daydream, or hint around about "someday." Your relationships will not progress past friendship because those are mission rules, and that's what allows the missionary to do his job. Missionaries refrain from daydreaming about romance for the same reasons. It's against the mission rules, and it prohibits them from doing their job as missionaries.

Consider your relationships with members of the opposite sex in which there is an age difference. For example, you girls probably don't foster romantic fantasies about younger boys because they generally don't make very good romantic partners. They make good friends, but girls usually choose a romantic partner their own age or older. These boy-girl friendships don't unavoidably lead to romance.

Remember Joey, the boy down the street with whom my daughter has been best friends since they were toddlers? All their friends thought they would make such a cute couple and pressured them to go together. However, my daughter never considered Joey as a potential romantic partner even as they grew older because Joey was a die-hard Catholic. He wasn't about to leave Catholicism any more than my daughter was about to leave the LDS Church.

Whether it's because the guy/girl is already taken, because work prohibits it, because the Church prohibits it, or because age differences or gender orientation make it unlikely, these are five instances where you can resist becoming romantic because you told yourself "no chance—don't even go there."

Of course there are disloyal humans who will prey on their same-gender friend's boyfriend or girlfriend. There are also sneaks who will try to break company rules and date people they work with. But for those honest folks, who know what's socially acceptable and morally right, you tell yourself you won't go there, and you don't.

Alternatives

Those of you who make a deliberate decision to avoid going steady during high school absolutely will have the capacity to resist romance during your teen years. This does, however, bring up the concern that you won't know what to do instead and you will avoid relationships with members of the opposite sex altogether.

It's healthy to have friendships with members of the opposite sex in high school and not necessary to avoid them all together. Since boy-girl friendships have so many benefits, it would be helpful to have some role models for those high school friendships that aren't necessarily headed for romance.

Unfortunately you can't depend on the media to provide good role models to prove that boys and girls can be friends without necessarily becoming romantic. From what I read, the credibility of television is completely shot. The so-called reality shows resemble anything but reality. Whenever you see a terrific friendship in the movies, it always ends up with a kiss, just before the credits roll.

The friendship in *Princess Diaries* is delightful at the beginning, but you can guess what happens at the end. Harry Potter films depict a wonderful friendship between Hermione and Ron. Only at the end, when they are almost out of Hogwarts (which appears to be the equivalent of high school), does romance blossom.

Because there are so few movies that depict good old-fashioned friendship between teenage boys and teenage girls, you may choose to rely on movies that begin with a good friendship to show you how to have a healthy boy-girl friendships. Just remember to pop out the DVD before the movie ends, lest you become convinced that friendships simply must turn into a romance.

There is nothing at all wrong with a friendship becoming a romance. As we have discussed in this book, healthy romances begin with a sound friendship. However, every friendship doesn't have to become a romance and won't necessarily become a romance. So you must know how to you relate to members of the opposite sex when you are not preparing for romance.

A potential paradigm for healthy boy-girl friendships sometimes appears in pre-adolescent movies. (At least it used to. These days, the media even has the pre-adolescents becoming romantic.) One of my favorite stories about a boy-girl friendship is *The Bridge to Terabithia,* in which a young girl shows a boy how to use his imagination to escape a troubled home life. Another likely candidate is *A Far off Place* with Reese Witherspoon, in which two preteens trek across a desert to escape their parents' murderers. (Sorry, I had to go back to 1993 to find a good example.) The Academy Award-winning movie *Hugo* is a more recent movie that depicts a healthy boy-girl friendship. You may tend to dismiss movies about pre-adolescents as having no merit because they are about children. However, these examples contain many of the elements of a genuine friendship, so if you want examples of really good friendships, pre-adolescent movies are a likely place to look.

Be the Role Model

In the end, you might be the best example of all. You might be the one your peers copy when they need a role model for a healthy boy-girl friendship.

I cannot find the exact version or the source for the following story, but I'll tell it to you the way I remember hearing it thirty-five years ago.

When I was in eighth grade, I transferred to a new school. Eager to fit in, I started watching the other boys, looking for someone to copy. Soon, I met a boy named Corky Savison, who seemed to be very popular. I started to walk like Corky Savison and talk like Corky Savison.

Before long, he changed. Corky Savison no longer walked and talked the same way. He began to walk and talk like Joey Havelin. He mixed me up. So I began walking and talking like Corky Savison's imitation of Joey Havelin.

As soon as I thought I had everything figured out, my idols changed again. Corky Savison no longer walked like Joey Havelin because Joey Havelin began to walk and talk like Billy Chambilin. Who the heck was Billy Chambilin? Why, that irritating little kid who is always trying to walk and talk like me!

High school students are continually looking for role models. Since you are now aware that friendship during the high school years can be lots of fun, less drama prone, and better for your social and emotional development than any other kind of boy-girl relationship, that role model might as well be you. Set the standard. Change the world. Be the first. You don't need anybody to model. Somebody else needs you.

Too often we rely on others to make decisions about

what is cool or popular. I was struck by the experience of Joshua Bell, a violin virtuoso who performed the Oscar-winning score for *The Red Violin*. Bell was asked to dress like a street performer and play his violin in a Washington DC subway during rush hour. In forty minutes' time, only a handful of people stopped to listen. Had there been a sign in front of his violin case, like there is in front of masterpiece paintings at an art museum, he would have been mobbed with people listening.

Don't wait for someone else in the high school to decide whether it is or isn't cool to get a boyfriend or girlfriend before graduation. Decide for yourself. Then show those who have long thought that obtaining a high school sweetheart was the ultimate quest, how much more comfortable boy-girl friendships can be.

Youth dances are a great place to show your peers how to act like friends act. Join in the line dances and the circle dances and the square dances . . . any of the dances where you don't drape your arms around one another's neck and lean your cheek on your partner's shoulder or hair. Dance with lots of different people, not just one. Talk to lots of different people, not just one. Sit with different people, not just one. Walk with different people, not just one.

Do the same thing wherever youth are gathered . . . at firesides, bonfires, treks, service projects, sporting events, movie nights, or youth conferences. Don't look around trying to identify one person to claim as your own, look around at all the people you can befriend during this opportune time of life.

I was speaking about unsteady dating at a youth conference in Las Vegas, Nevada, once, and the audience was unusually rapt. They stared straight ahead, silent as monks. At the end of the presentation, one of the adult leaders came up to me and explained the reason for their attention. Apparently several of the youth in the audience had come to the youth conference as couples. Many were sitting together, actually holding hands. If I had been standing closer to the audience, I could have seen perspiration break out on their brows as I continued my talk. To their eternal credit, these wonderful youth listened. They had faith to follow a prophet, and they put one another's hand aside.

When the group broke to attend their workshops, one particular couple met at the drinking fountain.

"What do you think?" the leader heard them say.

"It looks like we're just supposed to be friends."

"Not just friends, 'fabulous friends,'" was the response.

"Fabulous friends it is!" They raised their hands and slapped each other a high-five, and then they turned around and went to class.

You can do this. If you unknowingly entered into the steady dating stage while still in high school, back up. Agree to be fabulous friends, and each of you go and find others to go on dates with. If you've been lucky enough to form friendships with members of the opposite sex, keep those friendships! Don't rush into romance. High school friendships will last when romances fizzle. There is always time for romance after a mission. Don't rush it. Romance will not disappoint you if you wait until the time is right. If you are patient and wait, romance can be more fulfilling than you ever imagined.

Endnotes

1. Oscar Wilde, *Lady Windermere's Fan*, Act 2.

Appendix

EVERY STAGE OF A RELATIONSHIP HAS PHYSICAL behaviors that belong in that stage and are appropriate for that stage of the relationship. When people stick with the physical behaviors that are appropriate in that relationship stage, they can experience joy and fulfillment in their relationships. Too often people want to "cross the lines." In other words, they pair the wrong physical behavior with whatever stage their relationship is in. This type of mix-up leads to hurt feelings, anger, broken hearts, and sin.

Couples may pretend they don't need to keep the lines parallel, and they may believe no harm is done by crossing the lines. However, they discover that crossing the lines leads to misery, sometimes immediately, and sometimes as time passes.

Ideally, when a couple has integrity, and desires a successful relationship with both members of the couple getting the same satisfaction from the relationship, the connection between the relationship stage and the physical behavior looks like this:

APPROPRIATE MATCH BETWEEN PHYSICAL BEHAVIORS AND RELATIONSHIP STAGE		
Stage	Emotional Level	Physical Behavior
Stage 1	acquaintance	handshake
Stage 2	friends	high five
Stage 3	casual dating	brief hug
Stage 4	serious dating	hand-holding/brief kiss
Stage 5	engagement	lingering kiss/hug
Stage 6	marriage	intercourse

Five Ways to Cross an Acquaintance

There are over thirty ways to cross the lines, or in other words, mix up the emotional level of a relationship with the WRONG physical behavior. Following are ways people cross the lines.

Stage	Emotional Level	Physical Behavior
Stage 1	acquaintance ●	
Stage 2		● high five

If you had just barely met somebody, wouldn't you think it was a little weird if they suddenly started giving you a high-five as if you were already friends?

Stage	Emotional Level	Physical Behavior
Stage 1	acquaintance ●	
Stage 2		
Stage 3		● hugging

Hugging a stranger is a little uncomfortable. Perhaps if circumstances dictated, such as if you were at a ball game and you were sitting next to somebody who is as delighted about a big play you were it might not be out of place, but basically, it's just weird.

Stage	Emotional Level	Physical Behavior
Stage 1	acquaintance	
Stage 2		
Stage 3		
Stage 4		hand-holding/brief kiss

If you have just met someone and all of the sudden they are reaching for your hand and intertwining fingers, you would wonder if they were crazy. Maybe if you are with a tour guide who is helping you into a boat, you might want a stranger holding your hand, but not otherwise.

Stage	Emotional Level	Physical Behavior
Stage 1	acquaintance ●	
Stage 2		
Stage 3		
Stage 4		
Stage 5		● lingering kiss/hug

When two people who barely know one another make out, they are just using one another. You might consider such individuals extremely loose, or at the very least they have loose morals.

Stage	Emotional Level	Physical Behavior
Stage 1	acquaintance ●	
Stage 2		
Stage 3		
Stage 4		
Stage 5		
Stage 6		● intercourse

When two people who barely know one another have intercourse we call it a one-night-stand, or when money is exchanged, prostitution.

Five Ways to Cross a Friendship

Stage	Emotional Level	Physical Behavior
Stage 1		handshake
Stage 2	friendship	

In recent years, friends have begun to appropriately greet one another by shaking hands, but it's a different kind of handshake than the one you give a stranger. Frequently it will involve a fist bump, rotation of the hands to clasp thumbs, fingertip grip, and so on . . .

Stage	Emotional Level	Physical Behavior
Stage 1		
Stage 2	friendship	
Stage 3		brief hug

Crossing a friendship with a brief hug isn't weird if you really are friends. Casual dating is a friendship stage, after all. The awkwardness would occur if your date might misinterpret the hug and imagine you were pushing for a more serious relationship than they were ready for.

Stage	Emotional Level	Physical Behavior
Stage 1		
Stage 2	friendship ●	
Stage 3		
Stage 4		● hand-holding/brief kiss

This could truly be awkward if you go in for a kiss and your date just wants to be friends. It may seem nerdy to ask if it is okay to kiss your date, but this can be avoided if a couple simply discusses the level of their relationship.

Stage	Emotional Level	Physical Behavior
Stage 1		
Stage 2	friendship ●	
Stage 3		
Stage 4		
Stage 5		● lingering kiss

This inappropriate pairing is so common it actually has a name, "make-out buddy." Make no mistake, however, buddying up to someone just so you can make out is selfish, insensitive, and mean.

Stage	Emotional Level	Physical Behavior
Stage 1		
Stage 2	friendship ●	
Stage 3		
Stage 4		
Stage 5		
Stage 6		● intercourse

"Friends with benefits" is the deceptive term Satan's minions have slapped on this desecration of friendship. The only time friends should have intercourse is if they are also married.

Five Ways to Cross Casual Dating

Stage	Emotional Level	Physical Behavior
Stage 1		● handshake
Stage 2		
Stage 3	casual dating ●	

Shaking your date's hand at the end of a date might communicate that you didn't really enjoy the date all that much. It's rather businesslike and, unless you both laugh about it, might not communicate your true feelings about the date.

Stage	Emotional Level	Physical Behavior
Stage 1		
Stage 2		high five
Stage 3	casual dating	

Just like when you crossed a the physical behaviors of a friendship with the physical behaviors of casual dating, crossing the physical behaviors of casual dating with the physical behaviors of a friendship isn't much of a problem. Since casual dating is really a friendship stage, it's appropriate to act like friends act.

Stage	Emotional Level	Physical Behavior
Stage 1		
Stage 2		
Stage 3	casual dating	
Stage 4		hand-holding

This is the one of the most common way to cross the lines. Couples who know they aren't exclusive, and know they aren't committed engage in the physical behaviors that communicate exclusivity.

Stage	Emotional Level	Physical Behavior
Stage 1		
Stage 2		
Stage 3	casual dating	
Stage 4		
Stage 5		kissing

This is probably the next most common way to cross the lines. Couples who have no intention of staying together engage in physical behaviors that are appropriate only when there is a level of commitment. They may do it merely to satisfy their lusts.

Stage	Emotional Level	Physical Behavior
Stage 1		
Stage 2		
Stage 3	casual dating	
Stage 4		
Stage 5		
Stage 6		intercourse

This type of behavior can often qualify as "date rape," wherein one member of the couple has absolutely no intention of becoming sexual, but the other one coerces them, either verbally or physically, into having sex.

Five Ways to Cross Serious Dating

Stage	Emotional Level	Physical Behavior
Stage 1		● handshake
Stage 2		
Stage 3		
Stage 4	serious dating ●	

I can't imagine why, if you are seriously dating someone and thinking about marriage, you would shake his or her hand at the door step, unless you had previously experienced moral difficulty and an ecclesiastical leader was advising you to back off, way off. Otherwise, this behavior is simply prudish.

Stage	Emotional Level	Physical Behavior
Stage 1		
Stage 2		● high five
Stage 3		
Stage 4	serious dating ●	

Again, unless you've been instructed to be exceptionally careful, refusing to kiss the person you are considering marrying sounds like you're playing hard-to-get, or some other relationship game.

Stage	Emotional Level	Physical Behavior
Stage 1		
Stage 2		
Stage 3		brief hug
Stage 4	serious dating	

Only if you have both communicated to one another your apprehensions about the risk of excessive physical intimacy and a the risk of immorality, would this type of behavior be appropriate. Otherwise, it could be misunderstood, and appear as if you are merely a tease.

Stage	Emotional Level	Physical Behavior
Stage 1		
Stage 2		
Stage 3		
Stage 4	serious dating	
Stage 5		kissing/hugging

Just as the physical behaviors for casual dating stage are virtually identical to those of a friendship stage, the physical behaviors in a serious dating stage are similar to those of an engaged couple.

Stage	Emotional Level	Physical Behavior
Stage 1		
Stage 2		
Stage 3		
Stage 4	serious dating ●	
Stage 5		
Stage 6		● intercourse

The risk of intercourse in a serious dating relationship is extremely high. The exclusivity and commitment are present in the relationship, and the physical relationships can easily get out of hand. This is when it's extremely important to follow rules that focus on your physical interaction: don't put your hands where the bathing suit touches, don't be alone together, don't lie down next to one another, and so on. These are delineated beautifully on the lds.org website: https://www.lds.org/youth/video/chastity-what-are-the-limits?lang=eng

Five Ways to Cross an Engagement

Stage	Emotional Level	Physical Behavior
Stage 1		● handshake
Stage 2		
Stage 3		
Stage 4		
Stage 5	engagement ●	

If you have an engagement ring on your finger and a wedding date set and you are shaking hands, it sounds more like you are breaking up than getting married. If you're afraid of immorality, at least kiss her hand!

Stage	Emotional Level	Physical Behavior
Stage 1		
Stage 2		● high five
Stage 3		
Stage 4		
Stage 5	engagement ●	

While all the physical behaviors for stage one, two, three, and four relationships are appropriate in a stage-five relationship, the relationship would be suspect if you only experienced the physical intimacy appropriate in a stage one, two, three, and four relationship, without that appropriate for an engagement.

Stage	Emotional Level	Physical Behavior
Stage 1		
Stage 2		
Stage 3		brief hug
Stage 4		
Stage 5	engagement	

A hug is certainly welcome in the engagement stage, however, a willingness to be more physically intimate will bode well on the success of the eventual marriage.

Stage	Emotional Level	Physical Behavior
Stage 1		
Stage 2		
Stage 3		
Stage 4		kissing
Stage 5	engagement	

In some cultures, an engagement is as legally binding as a marriage. In our culture today, an engagement can be broken merely upon the agreement of the couple. Therefore, it's important to differentiate physical behaviors appropriate for those who are married from those appropriate for those who are not. Chances are the marriage may not occur.

Stage	Emotional Level	Physical Behavior
Stage 1		
Stage 2		
Stage 3		
Stage 4		
Stage 5	engagement ●	
Stage 6	●	intercourse

Oops! Because it's so easy to get too physical when you know you're getting married anyway, some couples choose to be extra cautious and stay as far away from temptation as possible. Therefore, even though kissing may be appropriate for a couple getting married, a couple who have decided together to be a little more cautious don't need to be considered prudish.

JeaNette G. Smith

Five Ways to Cross a Marriage

Stage	Emotional Level	Physical Behavior
Stage 1		handshake
Stage 2		
Stage 3		
Stage 4		
Stage 5		
Stage 6	marriage	

Just as inappropriate as intercourse is before marriage, it's often a sign of a troubled marriage when intercourse does not occur after marriage. If a married couple are merely shaking hands, it looks like they are headed for divorce.

Stage	Emotional Level	Physical Behavior
Stage 1		
Stage 2		high five
Stage 3		
Stage 4		
Stage 5		
Stage 6	marriage	

A high five is a gesture of affection so, as long as it is coupled with other more intimate gestures of affection, of course it is appropriate in a marriage.

Stage	Emotional Level	Physical Behavior
Stage 1		
Stage 2		
Stage 3		brief hug
Stage 4		
Stage 5		
Stage 6	marriage	

After all the discipline it took to put off intercourse until marriage, it seems unfathomable that married couples would merely give one another a hug. A surprising number of married couples choose not to take advantage of the fact that intercourse can help them become more emotionally intimate.

Stage	Emotional Level	Physical Behavior
Stage 1		
Stage 2		
Stage 3		
Stage 4		● hand-holding/kissing
Stage 5		
Stage 6	marriage ●	

This level of physical affection indicates that the marital friendship is intact. Couples can still bond with this level of intimacy.

Stage	Emotional Level	Physical Behavior
Stage 1		
Stage 2		
Stage 3		
Stage 4		
Stage 5		lingering kiss
Stage 6	marriage	

Couples may go through phases in the marriage when intercourse is restricted for various reasons, such as illness. Nevertheless, a marriage can stay strong where there is affection expressed in other ways.

Notes

About the Author

JEANETTE GOATES MARRIED BRET GERALD SMITH IN 1982, and they are the parents of four children and three grandchildren. They moved to Florida in 1988 where JeaNette pursued a master's degree in mental health counseling. Upon graduation, she became licensed as a marriage and family therapist and has spent the past eighteen years professionally helping couples and families. Her publications include three books, *Unsteady: What Every Parent Absolutely Must Know about Teenage Romance*; *Side by Side: Supporting a Spouse in Church Service*; and *From Playpens to Proving Grounds*, cowritten with her late father, Delbert T. Goates, MD. She speaks regularly at Brigham Young Campus Education Week and has spoken at the Brigham Young University Family Expo and the Families Under Fire Conference. She also has a talk-on-tape out: "No More Double Messages: Helping Adolescents Choose Abstinence." More information about JeaNette is available at www.smithfamilytherapy.org.